Second Edition

# THE DEATH OF HR
## Who Killed H.(HARRIET) R.(ROSE) Job?

Using Technology to gain **CLOUT**,
avoid career decline and
**empower** your HR Organization

Advice from an HR Technologist,
a Detective and an Alien visiting Earth

### Detective
## MARC S MILLER

For permission requests, write to the publisher, addressed "Attention: Permissions Coordinator," at the address below.

Publish Your Purpose Press

141 Weston Street, #155

Hartford, CT, 06141

The opinions expressed by the Author are not necessarily those held by Publish Your Purpose Press.

Ordering Information: Quantity sales and special discounts are available on quantity purchases by corporations, associations, and others. For details, contact the publisher at the address above.

Printed in the United States of America.

ISBN: 978-1-946384-44-7 (paperback)

ISBN: 978-1-946384-45-4 (ebook)

Library of Congress Control Number: 2018955465

Second edition, September 2018.

Publish Your Purpose Press works with authors, and aspiring authors, who have a story to tell and a brand to build. Do you have a book idea you would like us to consider publishing? Please visit PublishYourPurposePress.com for more information.

# Dedication and Purpose:

This book is dedicated to the community of HR and HR Technology professionals throughout the world who handle the challenging tasks of human capital management with, or without the help of technology and oftentimes without any recognition or realization by others (internally or externally), of the important role they play in any organization.

This book's sole purpose is to help HR and HR Technology professionals increase their own sphere of influence, their personal and professional **CLOUT**; and by doing so, increase the likelihood of new and strategic initiatives being implemented within the corporation to the benefit of all concerned.

# *What others are saying!*

"Death of HR" is a misnomer. HR already has enormous clout in many well managed companies. **This book is really about how businesses win through continued wise HR investments.** And, the book does a very nice job of laying out the source of this clout."

**DAVE ULRICH**
Rensis Likert Professor, Ross School of Business, University of Michigan
Partner, The RBL Group


"Harriet Rose (HR) is not dead. In fact, she is reborn, reinvented, and re-emerges as a strategic 21st Century Leader and master of collaboration. Marc Miller's unique and provocative book is **engaging, proactive, and serves as an essential read** to anyone managing in the vast global and virtual environment."

**YAEL ZOFI,** Virtual Teams Expert, Founder & CEO of AIM Strategies(R),
Author of A Manager's Guide to Virtual Teamst


"Marc Miller has written a book unlike anything I've read in the HR space. It's real, it's practical, it's fun; and yet it doesn't pull any punches (warning to the easily offended). This is a MUST READ for anyone who needs to understand "HR Value Add."

**MIKE GUGLIELMO**
Assistant Professor & Director of External Relations
Temple University | Fox School of Business
Human Resources Management Department


"With all the career disruption today, this book is a must read for every HR practitioner across the globe to avoid career suicide and help navigate the disrupted HR landscape and be prepared for the digital transformation that is coming our way. **I promise that you will laugh out loud more than once, too!**"

**ANNE FULTON,** Founder and CEO,
Fuel50 Career Pathing Software

# Acknowledgments and Thank You's

To my industry colleagues who have taken the time to review and provide comments, and to those who submitted endorsements:

| | |
|---|---|
| Roy Altman | Amy Heller |
| Phyllis Beasley | John McLaughlin |
| Robin Byers | Pam Puetz |
| Anne Fulton | Bob Schiff |
| Michael | Al Walker |
| Guglielmo | Carol Wiese |
| Julie Haak | Yael Zofi |
| Larry Hall | |

*A heartfelt thank you. You are all amazing!*

To my designer and editor, Allison Newsum – your creativity and your patience in helping me translate my ideas and source materials into this very readable book and into a fabulous reality – **WOW!**

To my family and friends who, although not knowing HR and HR Technology, provided insight and suggestions to help further clarify my content and message – another heartfelt *"Thank You" with hugs.*

# Who is
# H. (Harriet) R. (Rose) Job?

**This book presents Ms. H. R. Job as a real person,** the victim of a combination of workplace and personal issues that lead to the police investigation of her demise.

I am personalizing the overall function of Human Resources and its need to adapt to a variety of workplace challenges. How Ms. H. R. Job goes about her current role and how she is perceived by others and the extent to which she uses all possible personal characteristics and opportunities, such as her own **CLOUT**, or lack thereof – either self made or provided by her employer – is a metaphor for **the future effectiveness, if not survival, of the Human Resources function.**

# *Here's the premise upon which this narrative is built...*

I expect that readers of this book have an interest in the role of HR and its use of Technology, and most likely already use many forms of HR technology delivery within the organization. These applications can range from Recruiting to post retirement Benefits, from any number of HRMS providers and can be obtained from either a fully integrated capability or one that is focused on a single functionality ("best of breed"). Regardless of apporach there will always exist a multitude of date sensitive data items.

So there is *DATA and...*

- ❏ *Data* should lead to information
- ❏ *Information* could lead to influence
- ❏ *Influence* should lead to power
- ❏ *Power* and *influence* means *CLOUT*
- ❏ *CLOUT* should lead to **NEW** programs leading to personal and professional success!

Taking the initiative for your career, and avoiding becoming a "target", (like Ms. H. R. Job) is one critical objective for any level of HRJob. Thus, knowing your **CLOUT** level and then taking on some of the suggested "to-do" activities to maintain or increase your score and sphere of influence will further enhance your career.

Additionally, knowing how to use your **CLOUT**/influence properly will help you participate in, or manage global teams to maximum effectiveness, which will be duly noted by the top executives in your organization.

# Continuing the premise...

In the last few years (2016+), much has been discussed and written about the vast potential of Artificial Intelligence, both in main stream media and in journals related to almost every conceivable work function. Many writings more than speculate on the impact of AI on the role of Human Resources.

The goal of this book is to provide my readers knowledge and action items to further their career, enhance their status and help them anticipate new challenges. Artificial Intelligence can be deemed both a threat and a needed collaborating tool. By understanding and anticipating the impact of AI on HR's roles and responsibilities, it is hoped that you will embrace AI as vehicle for removing some of your own administrative burden, freeing you to seek and accomplish more strategic, value added initiatives which will serve as a shield of protection against being placed in a vulnerable position by others in your workforce, as Ms. H. R. Job was. (See the discussion in Part Five).

Additionally, as Supporting Material, I am providing important underlying concepts and information to keep you well informed of the latest trends in HR strategies, initiatives and outreach. If these newer roles are embraced by you the reader, your "Sphere of Influence" and **CLOUT** will surely be enhanced. The Supporting Material includes sample metrics and dashboard depictions, a suggested more visible role for HR in instilling awareness of Cyber Security threats to the Workforce of your organization, and a list of vendors who support and provide functionality to help employees take the initiative in managing and enabling their career within a corporation.

# You will find this book meaningful if you are...

❑ A **Senior Leader or Board member** of your organization – as it helps to set your expectation of the role and deliverables that can and should come from your HR function.

❑ A **Senior Leader of HR** in your organization.

❑ Any **Manager** or any level of staff within the function of HR in your company who wishes work activities were done more effectively and efficiently.

❑ **A HR technology service provider** who seeks a greater understanding of the issues and concerns among HR professionals - who might end up being a new prospect and eventually a customer.

# *Why this book could matter to you!*

❑ Provides you with specific action items to help you build your Sphere of Influence and **CLOUT** which will increase your personal and professional impact to further your advancement and avoid career decline.

❑ Points out the components and features of delivered HR Technology that instill **CLOUT**.

❑ Brings you up to date on how **HR technology** supports the business critical efforts of Human Resource professionals.

❑ Helps you to build your business case and gain executive sponsorship to any **HR Technology** initiatives by guiding you in how to show the value of your efforts to your C-Level executives.

❑ Suggests what the impact of **AI** can mean to the role and viability of any level of HR professional.

**While reading – keep in mind these quotations from Ginni Rometty – CEO of IBM Corporation:**

*"One of the most important things for any leader is to never let anyone else define who you are. And you define who you are. I never think of myself as being a woman CEO of this company. I think of myself as a steward of a great institution."*

*"I learned to always take on things I'd never done before. Growth and comfort do not coexist."*

**Additionally, this favorite quote of mine from one of the pioneers of Management Consulting, is one that strongly shapes this book:**

*"Information responsibility, then, begins with correctly identifying the information you need to effectively carry out your job, and extends to ensuring that the information flows to people in other areas who stand to benefit from it, and in a form in which those people will readily understand it.*

*"…Increasingly, however, the measure of the executive will **not be his/her ability to interpret data, but his/her ability to define and exploit information."***

Peter Drucker
"Across the Board"
December 1991

# Table of Contents

**Part One:**                                    2

The Death of Ms. Harriet Rose Job


**Part Two:**                                    36

Gaining CLOUT


**Part Three:**                                  74

Using your influence and leveraging
HR technology to enhance your Career


**Part Four:**                                   94

Working on a team and preserving
your sphere of influence and CLOUT


**Part Five:**                                   132

Staying vigilant and anticipating what is likely to
change in the next few years.


**Part Six:**                                    156

Supporting Materials

# Part One:
# THE DEATH
# OF
# MS. H. R. JOB

# Contents:

- ❏ Prologue: Ms. H.R. Job's Last Day
- ❏ Crime scene
- ❏ Police Reports and Detective notes
- ❏ Suspects
- ❏ Other "persons of interest"
- ❏ Why Ms. H.R. Job was targeted
- ❏ The Possible Motives
- ❏ The Culprits

# Prologue:
# Ms. H. R. Job's last day . . .

**It was a dark and stormy night** (always wanted to start a piece with that infamous opening line!) and Harriet Rose had slept poorly due to the lightning flashes that illuminated her sparsely furnished apartment and her half-eaten and now melted Ben & Jerry's Rocky Road. She struggled to get ready to walk to her office, just blocks away. She had a busy day ahead and lots on her mind. She was not a pleasant person most mornings. Leaving her home in a northeast city, Ms. H. R. Job walks the 8 city blocks to her office in a new gleaming glass sided office tower.

**As Harriet Rose Job walks she thinks about the various aspects of her work and personal life...**

*"Oh well – another day another dollar. I need to get my coffee and a muffin on the next corner. They usually have it waiting for me at 8:16 am. Great, I've got 2 more minutes to walk 1 more block, perfect.*

*Ok, needed that first sip of hot coffee. So, what is on my schedule today? Ok, I meet with that new guy – Arturo Intelligente – he seems to be a strange young man, a bit cold and impersonal, especially to me.*

*I have no idea why he wants to meet with me? Last time I saw him it was in passing and he was talking to the "big boss" something about algorithms and Bots - what's that about? How does it affect me in HR? Oh well, I guess I will find out.*

*Gosh, so many people are new around the office.*

*Mostly young kids... sadly only Bebe Boomer and I seem to be left hanging around.*

*Oh, I must remember to prepare the excel report for the my boss Hugh. No big deal. He thinks it's a difficult report. Nope, been doing the same report for 10 years – maybe I change a heading or 2 just to keep it interesting. He won't even notice. He's too busy networking – he tells me he is "socializing" and pushing for new HR initiatives. Ha! Nothing gets done around here anytime soon. He's lucky that I at least know where the manuals are and can show him policy documents and old spreadsheet reports.*

*After all, I am the only person in HR with 20 years plus.*

*Oh, darn, not happy about my performance rating. But I have to sign my appraisal by Friday. Will look at again later. Boy, this place has changed. Heard that we won't be doing annual performance appraisals anymore. Seems we're moving to quarterly check-ins – no biggie, I get the same increase every year.*

*Other than that, work as usual. No one bothers me. In fact, no one really comes by and talks to me at all. I am ok with that. Even the big boss sees me and just nods my way and keeps walking. Haven't spoken with him for years.*

*Gosh, this elevator is full! More young people! – all looking at their smartphones or wearing ear plugs. No one even says good morning any more.*

*I'll get through the day. Just have to remember to nod at colleagues and keep walking. That's what I do best.*

*(Harriet gets off the elevator, now walking towards her office…)*

*Hmm.. I see Mel Lenial and Sue "Sis" Stems talking with the boss. Oh oh... they are calling me over – what could they want?*

*Ah, they asked me about our HR data base. I tell them its fine and that I know each data element backwards and forwards and don't need anything new.*

(Harriet now sitting at her desk...)

*Ah, glad to sit at my desk and finish my coffee and get to my muffin. OK, let me see my in-box and calendar. Oh yes, I see a reminder email, about some late day conference that I was invited to attend by Señor Managemento – What's that about? I guess I will find out.*

**Why can't I just be left alone and do my normal regular time filling stuff."**

# The Crime Scene Police Report:

At 7:30 p.m. that same day Ms. H.R. Job was found by a member of the office cleaning staff who called 911. She was in her office, lying face down near her desk, **a mouse cord was wrapped around her neck** . . . near her body:

- ❏ stacks of paper reports, spreadsheets, manuals/binders,
- ❏ an appointment book
- ❏ a tipped over file cabinet
- ❏ a Performance Appraisal (unsigned)
- ❏ a flip phone

# The Crime Scene Police Report:

(subsequent investigative notes)

- ❑ No suicide note was found.
- ❑ Ms. H.R. Job lived alone.
- ❑ She was age 53.
- ❑ She worked at this company for 24 years and was promoted twice. Her last promotion was 11 years ago.
- ❑ Ms. H. R. Job was not particularly liked, but was accepted by her co-workers as being a "loner."

# Canvassing the crime scene:

Understanding what might have led to the crime

## WAS IT MURDER OR SUICIDE?

While Ms. H. R. Job was doing her job…the investigation uncovered many things that changed!

The work landscape has moved from a **Production-Based Industrial Economy** to an **Information Based** connected and frictionless economy!

… and changed some more…
**"Brick and Mortar" was disappearing!**

There is now a new emphasis on:

    ✓ Speed

    ✓ Flexibility

    ✓ Imagination

**And NOT on:**

✗ Size

✗ Structure

✗ Physical Assets

Ms. H. R. Job found herself working in the **"Knowledge Economy."**

As such, organizations require a workforce that exhibits and embraces a mindset that:

❏ Seeks **"Breakthroughs"**

❏ Desires **"Exploration"**

❏ Shows **"Mental Flexibility"**

❏ Is always **"Curious"**

❏ Is **"Creative"**

❏ Shows **"Nimble-ness"**

**MS. H. R. JOB HAD NONE OF THESE CHARACTERISTICS!**

And so, yes, in a KNOWLEDGE or "BRAIN-BASED ECONOMY," *BUREAUCRACY KILLS!*

In a "Brain-based economy," organizations that succeed and prosper:

- ❑ Deliver Market Leading, **Consumer Pleasing Products**

- ❑ Emphasize **Customer Service**

- ❑ Have **Speed to Market**

- ❑ Understand the **"Window of Opportunity"**

- ❑ Seek the **Imagination** of Workers (not just employees)

- ❑ Reward Ingenuity in Product Development and Marketing

- ❑ Provide their workers a **team based, but high pressure, risk taking environment**

- ❑ Provide their workforce **career enhancement opportunities**

**Success** comes to any Organization when it BEATS their competition in:

- ❑ **Building APPS** that have Life changing capabilities
  - ◆ **Frictionless and addictive qualities**

- ❑ Using **Social Media** internally and externally

- ❑ Providing "Cool" tools for day to day use – **attractive to Millennial workforce, creating "BUZZ"**

- ❑ Matching **Marketing strategies** to demographics of consumer demand

- ❑ Obtaining and Retaining **the best people to DO the above**

- ❑ **Retaining employees** seeking job enrichment and **who show a willingness to gain new skills**

Companies that have done this well and have had the **CLOUT** **(power)** to change the way we go about our business, learn and interact with others:

Google 🍎 f Ⓤ
amazon.com 🐦 NETFLIX

In today's marketplace **"Information"** (not DATA) gathered and transmitted seamlessly AND instantly without IT support is the **Most Valuable Currency of Business.**

# HR's Role

Use Technology to:

- [ ] **Free the People** . . . by empowering them!

- [ ] **Identify the People** that should be freed (only those willing to be empowered!)

- [ ] Perform, reform and seek to **reduce the Bureaucracy** by outsourcing non-core activities

- [ ] **Provide Strategic, Value-Added "Information"** to the "Decision Makers" at every level of the organization

# Ideally...

You don't give people smartphones/tablets/laptops and tell them what to use them for...

...you give them the **access** to the technologies and to the tools and let THEM devise the applications necessary to **add value** to an organization!

# Back to our crime

## WHO HAD THE MOST TO BENEFIT FROM MS. H. R. JOB'S DEMISE?

# Why was Ms. H. R. Job targeted?

## Clues:

She . . .

- [ ] was unwilling to change
- [ ] was not a team player
- [ ] was stuck in her time
- [ ] did not try to embrace **new technology**
- [ ] did not seek new ways to become more efficient
- [ ] did not share her expertise

# Suspects:

- ❏ Bennie Fits
- ❏ "Buzz" Provement
- ❏ Harry R. Is
- ❏ Hugh Resources
- ❏ Pai Roal
- ❏ Sue "Sis" Stems

# "PERSONS OF INTEREST"

## Others to be called down to the station house:

- ❏ Cher Holder
- ❏ Otto (OT) Sur-sing
- ❏ Ed Konomy
- ❏ Señor Juan Managemento
- ❏ Art I. Inteligente
- ❏ Mel Lenial
- ❏ Bebe Boomer
- ❏ Ted D'Venda
- ❏ Jay Comp Etition

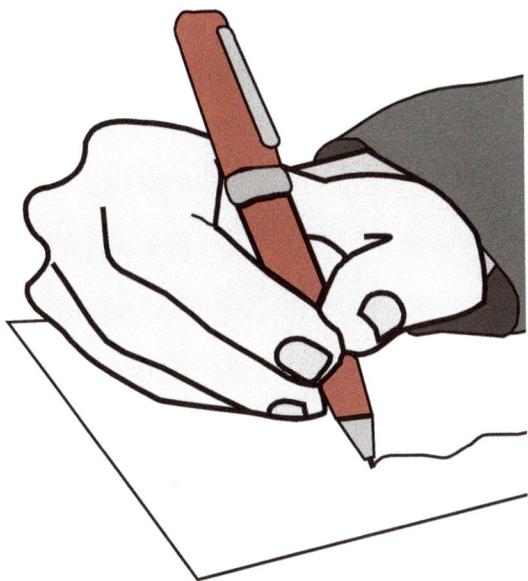

# Detective Miller's interview notes

Suspects and other persons of interest:
INTERVIEW NOTES, **QUOTES,** *& IMPRESSIONS*

---

# BEBE BOOMER

❑ liked to be considered a MENTOR –
Ms. H. R. Job assigned to be his mentoree -(NOTE)

❑ he stated **"she never listened"** ——————(QUOTE)

*Annoyed enough to do harm?* —— *(IMPRESSION)*

# MEL LENIAL

❑ Ms. H. R. Job considered **"old school"** – he
felt he was dealing with his **"grandmother"**,
and that she had "no patience."

*Maybe he wanted to get her out of
the way?*

# HUGH RESOURCES

❑ wanted **"young, energetic, nimble and
thoughtful staff"**, willing to market and sell
HR's role – Ms. H. R. Job was unable to do
any of this.

*Ms. H. R. Job reported to him, made him
look bad?*

---

# ART I INTELLEGENTE (AI)

❑ found Ms. H. R. Job too easy a target,
   **"easy to replace"**

*Wanted to get rid of her as low hanging fruit, and as a matter of due course?*


# TED D'VENDA

❑ **"could not grasp the importance of new technology, could not see the future vision, nor participate as a contributing member of an implementation team."**

❑ Team suffers, implementation goes badly. Venda reputation diminished.

*Wanted to get rid of her?*


# SUE "SIS" STEMS

❑ **"the company needed a new state-of-the-art HR technology."** Ms. H. R. Job was a vocal naysayer, and unwilling to support providing any new requirements. Stated that she was not "onboard" for any kind of change.

*She hated new technology.*

## BENNIE FITS and PAI ROAL

- ❑ both realized they were overburdened by inefficient workflow and spreadsheets and wanted better empowerment for all employees. Struggling to meet expanding workforce expectations and to improve employee engagement - wanted employee self service. Ms. H. R. Job not in support of making changes.

**Both did not like working with her!**

## CHER HOLDER

- ❑ "unfortunately our company is not showing value, not performing effectively and efficiently."

*Needed to send a strong message by getting rid of Ms. H. R. Job? Easy pickings?*

# OTTO (OT) SUR-SING

☐ wanted to take on the HR administration work. **"It makes no sense to me to having internal HR function keep it when technology and vendor can do it faster and cheaper."**

*Ms. H. R. Job was against this, thus targeted?*

# ED KONOMY

☐ **"Our company needs to stay as an "industry leader."** needed to position for survival and surpass others including Jay Comp Etition – who ran industry competitor and was close behind in market share. Needed to kill off inefficient and non-value adding people and processes.

*Ms. H. R. Job was targeted and an easy obstacle to remove?*

## BUZZ PROVEMENT

☐ **"Our organization and its processes are full of inconsistences and requiring multiple level of approval, unnecessary call center and old outdated policies and procedures."** Needed to clean house and smooth out many processes.

*Ms. H. R. Job was an obstacle?*

## SEÑOR JUAN MANAGEMENTO

☐ **"I am not happy with overall performance of our workforce, and I want more "value" and to see better stock performance."** Hugh Resources and Ms. H. R. Job not finding or building a good pipeline of talent. Feels workforce is overstaffed with "dead wood."

*Ms. H. R. Job targeted? Also sending a message to rest of workforce?*

# Why was Ms. H. R. Job targeted?

Her **MISTAKES** = the dreaded **5** "I"s

SHE WAS PERCEIVED BY COLLEAGUES AND
SENIOR MANAGEMENT AS BEING:

- ☐ **I**RRELEVENT
- ☐ **I**NDIFFERENT
- ☐ **I**NDECISIVE
- ☐ **I**NCOMPETENT, with no new skills
- ☐ **I**NFLEXIBLE

All **OBSTACLES** to her own,
and to her organization's
goals, vision, direction and
thus, success.

# Why was Ms. H. R. Job targeted?

Ms. H. R. Job, was an easy victim – she had **no CLOUT or influence,** nor any desire to fulfill her passion, nor did she pressure her organization to help her add value and increase her visibility and increase her sphere of influence.

And, she never took any initiative into her own hands, nor did she seize any opportunity to add visibility to her role… (see Part Six – for one such suggestion, that of co-leading the effort to **instill cyber threat awareness to the workforce.**)

# The possible motives?

**A summary from all Suspects and "Persons of Interest"**

- ☐ **Getting rid of any/all obstacles**

- ☐ For the "good of the Company"

- ☐ Seeking a more rewarding work experience

- ☐ Self preservation and survival

- ☐ Seeking personal Rewards and Recognition

- ☐ Wanting more Influence, Power – **CLOUT**

# The Culprits:

Who do you think killed Ms. H. R. Job?

## or was it SUICIDE?

# The Culprits:

## A Conspiracy...*all* participating

### ❑ Led By:

    ❑ Hugh Resources

    ❑ Harry R. Is

    ❑ Ted D'Venda

    ❑ Mel Lenial

### ❑ Masterminded By:

    ❑ Señor Juan Managemento

    ❑ Art Intelligente

# Will YOU be next?

A sixth **"I"** is needed.

To find out, a bit of **INTROSPECTION** is required:

☐ Are you able to embrace change in spite of what it might mean to your role and responsibilities?

☐ Can you effectively participate on a team whose objectives may result in a drastic change to your work or job?

☐ Do you know if your job is dying? Should it be? Is it better for the performance of your company?

☐ Do you work within an HR function that has no Clout or Influence with Senior Management?

IMPORTANTLY - WHAT OF YOUR
OWN LEVEL OF INFLUENCE AND
CLOUT?

*Let's FIND out* ➡

# Part Two:

# GAINING CLOUT

## AND AVOIDING CAREER DECLINE, SUICIDE OR BEING TARGETED

# Contents:

❑ What is **CLOUT**? Power or influence?

❑ Characteristics of people who have **CLOUT**

❑ Determining your **CLOUT** Level Score with the **CLOUT Determination Questionnaire**

❑ **CLOUT** and Ms. H. R. Job

# WHY YOUR UNDERSTANDING OF YOUR LEVEL OF INFLUENCE OR **CLOUT** IS NEEDED

PART TWO includes the latest version of my anecdotal, un-scientific 10 factor **CLOUT LEVEL DETERMINATION QUESTIONNAIRE.**

❑ By taking this QUESTIONNAIRE you will be conducting an **INTROSPECTIVE AND PERSONAL EXERCISE** that brings into focus where you might stand regarding your own **"sphere of influence"** within your organization. Importantly, it might lead you to taking responsibility for your own career management instead of relying solely on the opportunities offered to you by your organization.

❑ It moves you from being **a passive bystander**, to one of action, leading to greater utilization of your skills, passions, and capabilities.

❑ Once **YOU** learn your own **CLOUT Level**, you might undertake actions and initiatives to increase your level of influence, increases your own visibility, and use that new power to further **ENABLE your CAREER**. **Your own initiatives** combined with leveraging YOUR COMPANY'S HR TECHNOLOGY (HRMS) in support of LEARNING MANAGEMENT, CAREER ENABLEMENT AND PERFORMANCE MANAGEMENT FUNCTIONALITY will give you every opportunity to advance your career.

# Let's begin with what CLOUT is, and who has it?

Certainly – here in America, POTUS, by virtue of the title itself and the power granted to the POSITION (not the person) by our Constitution.

And globally, other Heads of State, by virtue of how they grasped, seized or shaped the way they rule.

*Also this person, named* ***"Klaatu"*** *. . . as we will see later.*

# But, it could be **you**....

and **it SHOULD BE YOU!**

# Definitions - **CLOUT**

## Webster's:

☐ A blow, especially with the hand

☐ A long powerful hit in baseball

## Informally **CLOUT** is conversationally referred to as:

☐ "Power"

☐ "Influence"

☐ "Pull"

☐ "Authority"

☐ "Sway"

☐ "Standing"

☐ "Muscle"

# The questions at hand:

- ❏ How do you get **CLOUT**? POWER?

- ❏ Do you already have some?

- ❏ What can you do to keep it? **(It is changeable)**

- ❏ What can your HR TECHNOLOGY do to give you POWER and **CLOUT**?

- ❏ Does an effective HR TECHNOLOGY bring **CLOUT**?

- ❏ Does having **CLOUT** facilitate bringing an effective HR TECHNOLOGY within the organization?

# HAVE YOU EXPERIENCED **CLOUT**? DO YOU HAVE IT?

Think about your life experiences – at work – at leisure – attending conferences – watching TV/movies, streaming shows, reading a mesmerizing book written by an author you have learned to seek out, listening to music, listening to an audible book, watching a TED Conference, etc. These activities remain in your mind because they impressed you, made you think, gave you enjoyment. It is quite possible your choice and even your memories have been influenced by a **"CLOUT-full"** person, an object, or a brand, creating an emotional response in you.

We all remember specific people in specific settings. Our memories are shaped by our feelings about people in terms of a few factors: are they doing or saying something that we personally value, relate to, understand or make us think about? Do they make other people take notice? When they enter a room or join a conversation do others pause to take note of their presence or what they are saying or

# HAVE YOU EXPERIENCED **CLOUT**? DO YOU HAVE IT?

doing? If you can remember a situation that you were in where these things happened, I would suggest you were in the sphere of influence of a person with **CLOUT**.

People who have **CLOUT** in their spheres of influence – in real life or in popular culture wield their power and influence to shape deals that THEY want, demand salaries and concessions that THEY want, and, in general, by the fact that they have power and influence and hence **CLOUT**, do indeed shape opinions and influence the actions of others.

They have their **CLOUT**, POWER OR INFLUENCE AS A DIRECT RESULT OF THE CLASSICAL SOURCES OF POWER:......

# PEOPLE GAIN **CLOUT** in many ways by having:

- ❏ "Formal" Authority

- ❏ control of Scarce Resources

- ❏ control of Decision Processes

- ❏ control of Knowledge and Information

- ❏ control of the Dissemination of said Knowledge

- ❏ control of Technology

- ❏ control of Boundaries

- ❏ strong Interpersonal Alliances, Networks

- ❏ control of the "Informal Organization"

# People with **CLOUT** HAVE:

☐ the ability or official capacity to exercise control, authority, to wield influence, to perform effectively. They gain their status by having any one or combination of these 5 types of power:

- **Reward Power** – controlling the allocation of rewards and incentives
- **Legitimate Power** - derived from the person's position, experience and status – by title
- **Coercive Power**- by having the ability to threaten, punish and exert potential damaging effects
- **Referent Power** - by having the respect, positive emotional bond over another person
- **Expert Power** -  by virtue as being seen by others as having strong expertise and experience

☐ the right or prerogative of determining, ruling, governing, or the exercise of that right or prerogative.

☐ the ability to shape or effect results.

IN MY OPINION, THE FOLLOWING ARE PEOPLE IN VARYING REALMS OF PROFESSIONS (REAL OR IN FICTITIOUS POP CULTURE) WHO POSSESS STRONG POWER, INFLUENCE – OR **CLOUT**......

# These people have **CLOUT** in their "spheres of influence" – in real life or in popular culture...

## BUSINESS
**Bill Gates,** Microsoft
**Warren Buffet,** Berkshire Hathaway
**Elon Musk,** SpaceX, Tesla Motors
**Mary Barra,** GM
**Jamie Dimon,** JPMorganChase
**Rupurt Murdoch,** CEO – News Corporation, 20th Century Fox,
**Bob Iger,** Walt Disney Company

## TV/MOVIES – ACTORS and their ROLES
**Marlon Brando** – The Godfather
**James Gandolfino** – Tony Soprano
**Jimmy Fallon, Stephen Colbert**
**Denzel Washington, Jennifer Lawrence, Tom Hanks**

## CABLE TV News
**Anderson Cooper, Sean Hannity, David Muir, Andrew Lack**
(Chairman NBC News), **Megyn Kelly, Samantha Bee, Bill Maher,**

## FILM/THEATER/ TV PRODUCTION
**Steven Spielberg, Lin-Manuel Miranda, Aaron Sorkin, Martin Scorsese, James Cameron, Judd Apatow, Ben Affleck, Ellen DeGeneres, Shonda Rhimes, Jeffrey Katzenberg, Oprah Winfrey**

## LITERATURE/AUTHORS
**Stephen King, James Pattterson, J.K. Rowling**

## POLITICS
**POTUS, Speaker of the House, Governors, Supreme Court Justices**

## TECHNOLOGY
**Mark Zuckerberg,** Facebook
**Sergey Brin/Larry Page,** Google Founders
**Tim Cook,** CEO, Apple
**Jeff Bezos,** CEO, Amazon

## HR
**Dave Ulrich,** Founder RBL Group
**Josh Bersin,** Founder, Bersin Deloitte Consulting

## HR TECHNOLOGY
**Dave Duffield,** Workday
**Dave Ossip,** Ceridian
**Scott Scherr,** Ultimate Software
Consultants: **Naomi Bloom, Jason Averbook, Marc Miller**

## SPORTS
**Lebron James,** basketball professional
**Roger Goodell,** NFL Commissioner
**Serena Williams,** tennis professional

# Characteristics of people with **CLOUT**

## What do they have?

- ❏ **People Insight** – Ability to read and understand those you come into contact with, at every level

- ❏ **Smarts** - Without intelligence, your **CLOUT**/POWER will be limited.

- ❏ Determination, **confidence**, self awareness

- ❏ Directed **energy**  - influencing others

- ❏ Ruthless **single-mindedness**

- ❏ **Skills in delegation** and motivation, thus "leadership"

- ❏ Corporate-intrigue **survival skills** – politics – a knowledge of the formal and **informal** political culture within the organization.

# What do they have to help wield **CLOUT**?

## More of what people have. . .

☐ **Benign deviousness**, a "player"

☐ **Risk taker,** aggressively, not passively

☐ **Health awareness**

☐ Effective **time management**

☐ Good **judgment**

☐ Ability to **"Sloganize"**

- ♦ Leaders create or adapt slogans that:
  - ▪ inspire others
  - ▪ communicate the organization

- ♦ An early example – the one word slogan **"THINK"** used by IBM founder Thomas J. Watson in 1920-1930's.

- ♦ GEICO – "15 minutes could save you 15% or more."

# Ability to, or belief in "sloganizing"

Miller's General-Purpose **CLOUT** Gaining
**Slogan Generator** – pick a 3 digit # 000-999

| <u>a</u> | <u>b</u> | <u>c</u> |
|---|---|---|
| 0 integrated | 0 management | 0 system |
| 1 total | 1 organizational | 1 initiative |
| 2 systematized | 2 integrated | 2 workflow |
| 3 global | 3 reciprocal | 3 shift |
| 4 functional | 4 web-based | 4 policy |
| 5 visionary | 5 logistical | 5 concept |
| 6 cloud-based | 6 transitional | 6 project |
| 7 predictive | 7 incremental | 7 analytics |
| 8 compatible | 8 frictionless | 8 application |
| 9 crowd sourced | 9 transactional | 9 initiative |

*(Source: Adapted from "The Baffle-Gab Thesaurus," "The Buzz Phrase Projector," and "The Handy Obfuscator.")*

e.g. **"344"** – "global web-based policy"
**A perfect slogan!**

# Characteristics of People With Clout

People with **CLOUT** understand
the difference between
*Efficiency vs. Effectiveness*

Efficiency is often confused with effectiveness.
*But it is easy to be 100 percent efficient and
0 percent effective!*

| Efficiency | versus | Effectiveness |
| --- | --- | --- |
| do things right | rather than | do right things |
| solve problems | rather than | produce alternatives |
| safeguard resources | rather than | optimize resources |
| follow duties | rather than | obtain results |
| lower costs | rather than | increase profits |
| select HR tech on time | rather than | select right HR Tech |
| implement HRT on time | rather than | satisfy users |
| produce current status reports | rather than | strategic value reports |

# Company "Politics" and Power

☐ People with **CLOUT** understand the nature of "politicking" in the environment they work in. They are AWARE of their surroundings in the workplace.

☐ People with **CLOUT** are aware of their company's **POWER PROFILE**… both formal power and informal power structures, which is a critical component of the organizations' **"CULTURE"** and the nature of "Politicking" within the daily practices in the organization.

For example, is "IN-FIGHTING" . . .

…discouraged and not rewarded?

…accepted – as the way "it is"?

…played by nearly everyone to an ex.

# "Politics" and Power

Your potential as a person with **CLOUT** and **POWER** is based on your need for:

- ☐ Dominance over others
- ☐ Affiliation
- ☐ Control of situations
- ☐ Achievement
- ☐ Attention
- ☐ Increased competence
- ☐ Ego-building responses
- ☐ Aggression

- ☐ Status and prestige
- ☐ Independence
- ☐ Recognition
- ☐ Self-esteem
- ☐ Dependence
- ☐ Failure avoidance
- ☐ Risk taking
- ☐ Being liked by peers
- ☐ Social Interaction

So,

☐ Everyone wants some kind of power!

☐ But sometimes we do not understand or anticipate the **DISRUPTIVE EFFECT** that seeking power has on projects. That of creating **CONFLICT** which can easily make any project fail.

☐ Everyone wants to feel they have some sort of **CLOUT** and INFLUENCE in both their personal and work life.

Let's find out yours . . .

# Determining Your Own Clout Level -
## Here are the components . . .

**FACTOR 1:** Personal Influence

**FACTOR 2:** Influential HRT

**FACTOR 3:** HRT support of Business

**FACTOR 4:** Ten Management
   Potential Questions

**FACTOR 5:** Job Title (formal)

**FACTOR 6:** Proximity to M.S.P.

**FACTOR 7:** Well Roundedness

**FACTOR 8:** Political Savvy

**FACTOR 9:** Force of Personality

**FACTOR 10:** Longtime "F.O.B(oss)" Status

# FACTOR 1:
## YOUR PERSONAL INFLUENCE

Think about yourself when answering these questions.

Keep track of your "yes" answers to the following ten questions:

1. Do you react with integrity, dignity, fairness, and empathy for others in both positive and negative circumstances?

2. Are you unwilling to accomplish personal objectives at the expense of the company or others?

3. Do you have relationships with people representing a variety of knowledge bases throughout the organization, industry, and/or community?

4. Are you asked to be involved in situations outside of YOUR functional area or above YOUR level in the organizational hierarchy?

5. Do you shine the "spotlight" on others making sure they receive credit for accomplishments?

Factor 1: continued

6. Do you consistently produce results?

7. Do you associate during work and personal time with others who are known to be powerful/influential in the company, industry and/or community?

8. Do you willingly share resources?

9. Do you interact well with all types of people at all levels in the organization?

10. Do you seem to be able to instill confidence in others, by mentoring or acting as a sounding board?

## Factor 1 Score

Of the 10 statements shown in these last 2 **PAGES**:

How many (first impression) "yes" answers? ____

Give yourself 10 points for each "yes"      x 10

### Total Factor 1 score: ____

Maximum – 100 pts,
Minimum – 50 points (even if none)

# FACTOR 2:
## Characteristics of an "Influential" (Clout-full) HR Technology Environment

## Characteristics of the System Itself and Its Administration:

**10 statements follow – keep track of the number that describes your current HR technology environment**

1. WEB delivered, SaaS

2. ESS and MSS integrated – Manager "In-Box"

3. Smartphone/Tablet applications available or enabled

4. Metrics – Business Intelligence (beyond simple reports)

5. Metrics presented as a graphical Dashboard

6. Workflow built in, Emails, templates, trigger events, default approvals, Life Cycle changes pushed directly to employee and manager.

7. Single sign-on within multiple functional modules, including On-Boarding, Payroll, Benefits Administration, etc.

Factor 2: continued

## FACTOR 2:
Characteristics of an "Influential" (Clout-full) HR Technology Environment

8. Modeling and forecast projections of some key metrics, such as "future Turnover".

9. Third party Vendor(s) provides what is not among your company's core competencies.

10. Real time, Payroll calculation, ability for "on the go" adjustments and rerun of payroll calculation – even including time entry.

### Factor 2 Score

**Based on the 10 factors identified as an "effective or Clout-full HR Technology:**

If you believe that your CURRENT ENVIRONMENT HAS **8 OR MORE** of these factors................300 PTS

If you believe that your CURRENT ENVIRONMENT HAS **5 – 7** of these factors........................200 PTS

If you believe that your CURRENT ENVIRONMENT HAS **1-4** of these factors.......................... 100 PTS

If you believe that your CURRENT ENVIRONMENT HAS **NONE** of these factors......................... 50 PTS

### Total Factor 2 score: _____

# FACTOR 3:
How does your current HR technology support the BUSINESS of your company?

## What does your Business need from HR Technology?

Here are 5 abilities of HR technology, how many does your current system accomplish:

1. An HRT must provide information about productivity of the workforce and provide strategic value – added **information (not data)** about the competencies and performance of all staff.

2. An HRT should have the ability to forecast, model, and present results as a graphical metric showing trends – into the future.

3. The HRT must provide information to support the (known by HR) strategic plans of the business.

4. The HRT must easily accommodate changing organizational structure.

5. The HRT must strongly assist in the identification of "key employees" and the overall talent management initiatives within the company.

Factor 3: continued

# FACTOR 3:

## How does your current HR technology support the BUSINESS of your company?

What Does Business Need from HRT?

## Factor 3 Score

Of the 5 statements on the previous page, how many can you say that your HR technology can provide and thus be influential in shaping strategic decisions?

> Give yourself 100 points for each of the five you seem confident that your HR technology can do today.
>
> MAXIMUM – 500 POINTS
> MINIMUM – 100 POINTS (FOR PARTICIPATING)

## Total Factor 3 score: _____

## FACTOR 4:
### YOUR MANAGEMENT POTENTIAL AND PERSONAL FACTORS IN **10 QUESTIONS**

1. Can you name the 2 companies your CEO **POINTS** considers to be his/her most admired?

    Yes .................................................. 50pts

    No .................................................. 10pts \_\_\_\_\_

2. Do you know (and would your CEO agree) your company's top competitor(s)?

    Yes .................................................. 5O pts

    No .................................................. 10 pts \_\_\_\_\_

3. In the last year alone, have you marketed your HR systems' capabilities within your company by doing any of the following:

    • Speech or presentation to managers

    • Survey of employees or managers and follow-up

    • Published anything describing your capabilities – brochure etc.

    • Distributed any reports/METRICS/ DASHBOARDS to your executive leadership – with or without their request.

    **Yes (if many or similar efforts executed) .. 50 pts**

    No .................................................. 10 pts \_\_\_\_\_

4. Do you know your company's level of sales or revenue for the past full accounting year, **or at least the up or down trend?**

    Yes .................................................. 5O pts

    No .................................................. 10 pts \_\_\_\_\_

Factor 4: continued ▶

## FACTOR 4:
### YOUR MANAGEMENT POTENTIAL AND PERSONAL FACTORS IN **10 QUESTIONS**

**POINTS**

5. When asked for information do you provide it based on:

    Current data only ............................... 10 pts

    Current and Historical ......................... 30 pts

    Current and Future ............................ 60 pts  _____

6. Is your office on the same floor (in same building) as:

    Your boss ......................................... 20 pts

    Most Senior Person in HR ................... 50 pts

    CEO/President ...................................100 pts

    Anywhere else in the building............. 10 pts

    Work remotely ................................... 40 pts  _____

7. With whom is the highest level meeting that your regularly attend?

    Senior VP or above ......................... 200 pts

    VP ................................................. 100 pts

    Director .......................................... 70 pts

    Manager ......................................... 50 pts

    Anyone else .................................... 10 pts  _____

8. Most of your important (strategic) meetings are in the:

    Boardroom ...................................... 50 pts

    Boss's Office ................................... 40 pts

    Conference Room ............................ 30 pts

    Your Office ...................................... 20 pts

    Cafeteria ........................................ 10 pts  _____

## FACTOR 4:
### YOUR MANAGEMENT POTENTIAL AND PERSONAL FACTORS IN **10 QUESTIONS**

9. Are you on any formal management level committee?

> Yes ................................................... 50 pts
>
> No ................................................... 20 pts  _____

10. The size of your HR/Payroll Master File with active records

> Greater than 5000 active records .......... 200 pts
>
> Between 1000 and 4999 active records .. 100 pts
>
> Between 500 and 999 active records ...... 50 pts
>
> Less than 500 active records ................... 5 pts  _____
>
> **Note: If you are a solo-prenuer (consultant or "gig" employee), or if you work in any size company as an individual contributor, or if your own company has less than 200 records – give yourself 100 pts**

**BONUS:** If you are administering within your  _____
system any active records in a foreign location

> ADD .............................................100 pts

## TOTAL FACTOR SCORE:  _____
MIN 105 pts ... MAX 960 pts

## FACTOR 5:
### YOUR CURRENT JOB TITLE

Chief HR Officer / President / Founder..........500 pts

Senior VP,EVP and above ........................ 400 pts

VP OR Director  (or Project Director)............. 300 pts

Manager (or Project Manager) .................. 200 pts

All else ................................................ 100 pts

If you are a Solopreneur ......................... 300 pts

**Total Factor 5 score:** _____


## FACTOR 6:
### YOUR PROXIMITY TO THE MOST SENIOR PERSON (MSP) IN YOUR ORGANIZATION

YOU are the MSP........................................ 300 pts

MSP is 1 level above your job title level
(you are next in line) ................................. 250 pts

MSP is 2 levels above................................ 200 pts

MSP is 3 levels above ................................ 100 pts

**Total Factor 6 score:** _____

# FACTOR 7:
## WELL ROUNDEDNESS, QUALITY OF INTELLECT, HOBBIES, ETC.

The total number of the following activities that you accomplished in the last **TWO YEARS**:

- ❐ read a number of "literary books"
- ❐ seen a number of "independent" films
- ❐ attended Operas or Shows
- ❐ visited Museums
- ❐ read any number of books/journals in your field of interest
- ❐ spent time on your hobbies (at least a few hours a month)

If **greater than 10** such activities ...............100 pts

If **between 6-9** such activities ..................... 90 pts

If **between 1 and 5** such activities ............. 70 pts

If **NO Activities** like these ........................ 50 pts

**Total Factor 7 score:** _____

# FACTOR 8:
## POLITICAL SAVVY – CORPORATE SURVIVAL,
### ABILITY TO HANDLE YOURSELF IN INTERNAL STRUGGLES

The number of reorganizations, Reductions In Force, or other kinds of downsizing you have survived – during your career:

if NONE ............................................... 50 pts

if ONE ............................................... 100 pts

if MORE THAN ONE ............................ 200 pts

**Total Factor 8 score:** _____

# FACTOR 9:
## FORCE OF YOUR PERSONALITY

During the last year, think of the number of significant disagreements you have had (or arguments): then choose your answer:

I usually WIN more arguments/disagreements than not – both in my personal life and my work life .......... 100 pts

I usually have had more success "winning" at work than when involved with personal life......................... 80 pts

I usually have had more successes "winning" in my personal life than I do in work situations .............. 50 pts

If NONE OF THIS applies, or you cannot decide..75 pts

**Total Factor 9 score:** _____

# FACTOR 10:
## LONGTIME "F" "O" "B" – FRIEND OF BOSS

### Statement 1:
You knew your boss prior to his/her accession, or prior to your current position or job

### Statement 2:
He (or She ) is (or was) considered by you to be a social friend or mentor

### SCORING:

If **YES** to **both** statements...................... 50 pts

If **YES** to **one** statement ........................ 40 pts

If **none** apply .................................... 10 pts

### Total Factor 10 score: _____

# Determining Your Own Clout Level - Worksheet

**FACTOR 1:** Personal Influence _____

**FACTOR 2:** Influential HRT _____

**FACTOR 3:** HRT support of Bus _____

**FACTOR 4:** Ten Management
           Potential Questions _____

**FACTOR 5:** Job Title (formal) _____

**FACTOR 6:** Proximity to M.S.P. _____

**FACTOR 7:** Well Roundedness _____

**FACTOR 8:** Political Savvy _____

**FACTOR 9:** Force of Personality _____

**FACTOR 10:** Longtime "F.O.B(oss)" Status _____

TOTAL CLOUT SCORE
*RAW SCORE 665 - 3110* _____

Round to closest 100 _____

# WHAT YOUR SCORE MEANS

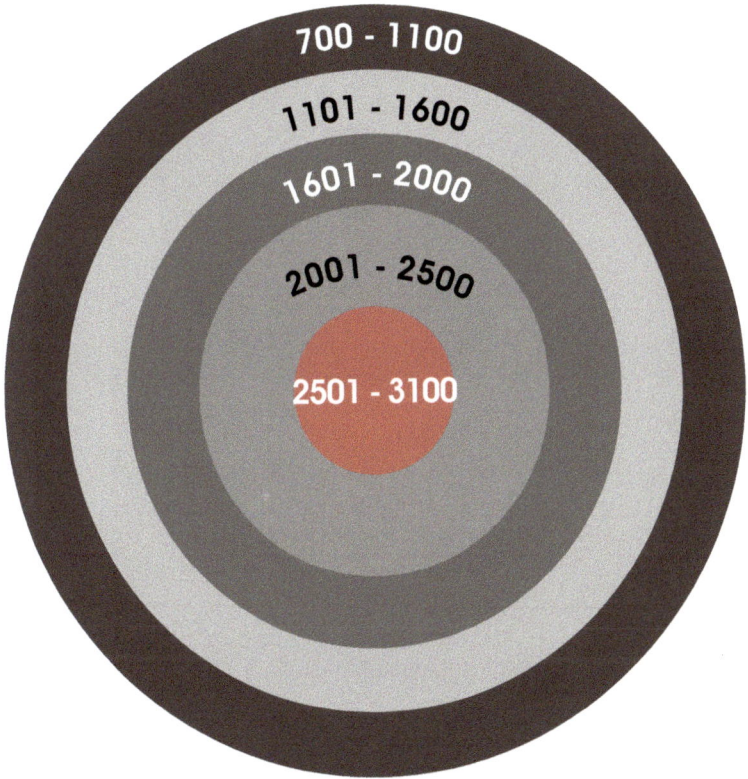

700 - 1100

1101 - 1600

1601 - 2000

2001 - 2500

2501 - 3100

Place your total score here _____

# WHAT YOUR SCORE MEANS

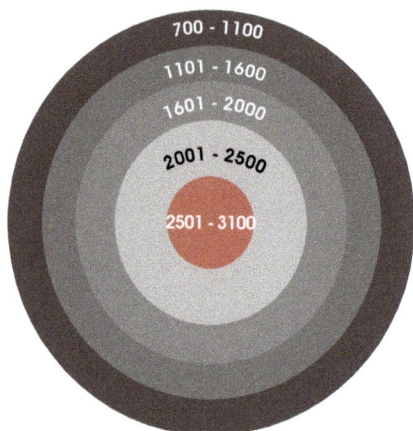

**HIGH CLOUT**

**NO CLOUT**

### 2501 - 3100
A member of the "INNER CIRCLE" to M.S.P – (Most Senior Person) you are routinely providing counsel

### 2001 - 2500
A great amount – your opinion is sought out and considered

### 1601 - 2000
Approaching influence – your opinion is listened to

### 1101-1600
Senior leadership might recognize your face and know your name without prompting

### 700 -1100
Boss might recognize you as being a member of the workforce

# Back to our crime . . .

If Ms. H. R. Job had taken our **CLOUT survey** we could have anticipated that with little or no **CLOUT, she would have scored near 1,000 points only**. Thus was no match for anyone who wanted her "gone", and she had no internal cadre of "protectionists," no one to stand up for what she does or had accomplished over the years.

**We now know (after investigating) that she never took any initiative, nor seized any new opportunities.** And she never indicated she understood the **"big picture"** of her company. She stayed in the safety of the **silo** of her administrative activities – in which she was comfortable.

# Part Three:

# AWARENESS,

# SELF DEFENSE

# AND CAREER GROWTH

BUILDING YOUR PERSONAL
AND PROFESSIONAL **CLOUT** AND
INCREASING YOUR POWER AND
INFLUENCE... SO YOU WILL NEVER
BE TARGETED

# Contents:

❏ COMPONENTS OF "CLOUT-FULL" HR TECHNOLOGY

❏ Moving from data management to information craftsmanship: your role and use of HR and HR Technology to deliver value added information that is in alignment with your organization

❏ How to market yourself and your system capabilities: "to-do" lists for HR and HR Technology staff

This section provides the underlying **mindset and action items to all HR Technologists and/or HR workforce members.**

It explores and suggests the neccessary **CLOUT** building approaches that helps to **link** yourself and your HR technology to the **business of HR** and to your organizations' overall missions.

To do so, you must:

❑ understand the needs of the CEO/Board of Directors

❑ prove to the CEO that the HR Function:

   ♦ Provides information for strategic decisions

   ♦ Facilitates change as a result of strategic decisions

   ♦ Provides policies/programs that empirically benefit the bottom line and drive engagement

And thus, the function of Human Resources **DESERVES to be and MUST be** represented AT C-LEVEL – Executive Committee – strategic planning decisions – affecting the entire organization.

Your function must become
an expert at providing
**"Value added" information**.
and not just **static data**:

|  | Static Analysis | Strategic Support |
|---|---|---|
| **Data** | Static, Aging, Reactive, Transaction-based | Forward View: Projections and Forecasts, Delivery of Model-based metrics |
| **Costs** | Evaluate costs already spent | Future costs estimated Future value estimated |
| **Analysis** | Current Workforce: status, current and historical transactions at single point in time | Estimating future totals and formulating scenarios using projections based on historical trends |

## YOU MUST TRANSITION FROM
"Data Management" to "Information Craftsmanship"

# HR Executives must anticipate and then answer **Strategic questions** – such as these:

☐ How do we know who our "key" people are? How do we keep them? If a "key" person leaves – who is available to replace that person?

☐ How many of our most effective managers will leave voluntarily or retire in each of the next 5 years? What will be the cost to recruit, train, and retain replacements?

☐ What is the impact of our relocating to a suburban location? How many employees would most likely commute? Could we forecast turnover as a result? Who and how many are likely to leave, and at what cost?

And this, one of the most succinct strategic questions (in my opinion), ever asked by a CEO to his C-Level advisory board:

☐ **"What country do we get into next, and what do we do there?" – Cargill CEO (2007)**

We in HR and HR Technology must know how the **BUSINESS of HR** and the overall company is performing!

Every program within the HR function must be viewed in terms of its:

☐ Cost effectiveness and ROI

☐ Ability to improve workforce efficiencies

☐ Utilization by the workforce: do they embrace it and understand its purpose?

☐ Impact on the overall strategy of the entity

# Linking HR and HR TECHNOLOGY to Your Business

## The product of HR and its use of technology is **Information**!

To make most strategic decisions, the Board of Directors, CEO, Executive Committee, CHRO, and other C-Level executives need **information** on:

- ❏ Products and cost of production
- ❏ Overhead
- ❏ Economic indicators
- ❏ Organizational financials
- ❏ Organizational structure
- ❏ The workforce and its utilization
- ❏ The marketplace
- ❏ Level of customer satisfaction
- ❏ Competitors
- ❏ Acquisitions and mergers
- ❏ Research and development
- ❏ Technology advances
- ❏ Human Resource programs and measurement

# HR must continue to evolve . . .

. . . and move from the role of "Administrator" to that of "Expert."

**EXPERT**

Strategic Expertise

⇧

Apply behavioral science knowledge for recruiting, evaluating, compensation, training, change management and perform workforce modeling and forecasts

**ENFORCER**

Control and Compliance

⇧

**ADMINISTRATOR**

Basic Personnel Services

⇧

Take a business perspective in compensation, benefits, recruiting and staffing, succession planning

Aspects of dealing with unions (1930s and 1940s in U.S.)

Bureaucratic and administrative aspects of dealing with employees - PERSONNEL

Dealing with discrimination and other US Federal Legislations - (1960s till present day)

Organizational effectiveness, business planning, workflow, best practices

**A VERY LONG TIME AGO**

**A WHILE AGO**

**RECENTLY – LAST 5-10 YEARS**

The evolution of HR must be accomplished by the utilization of a Value adding **CLOUT-FULL** technology having the following "value generating" components:

- ❑ Employee & Manager Self-Service (ESS/MSS)
- ❑ Forecasts & Trends via Dashboards
- ❑ Integrated HR/Payroll/Benefits functionality
- ❑ Web-delivered:
  - ◆ OnBoarding and Recruitment
  - ◆ Time Capture & Reporting
  - ◆ Performance & Career Development
  - ◆ Pay Calculation
- ❑ Web-delivered:
  - ◆ Work Group Collaboration
  - ◆ Workflow and best practices
  - ◆ Templates/Table resident text to populate most alerts and performance evaluation scoring/commentary
- ❑ Integration with Social Media sites
- ❑ "Best Practice" based functionalty and workflow
- ❑ Effective and attractive User Interface
- ❑ Single Sign-on

# **Value** is perceived as:

- ❏ Cost Reduction
- ❏ Cycle Time Reduction – Processing Efficiencies
- ❏ Improved Information – anticipatory and of strategic value
- ❏ Full Governmental Compliance at all levels
- ❏ Increased Capabilities & Functionality – in support of the workforce at all locations for all types of contributors and for all working "generations"
- ❏ Enhanced **Employee Engagement** based on strong adaptability of delivered functionality
- ❏ Data Quality at 100%
- ❏ "Big Picture" – Business Metrics easily available

Although still needed to accomplish daily tactical and regulatory tasks, HR needs to seek a new level of **INFLUENCE/value**.

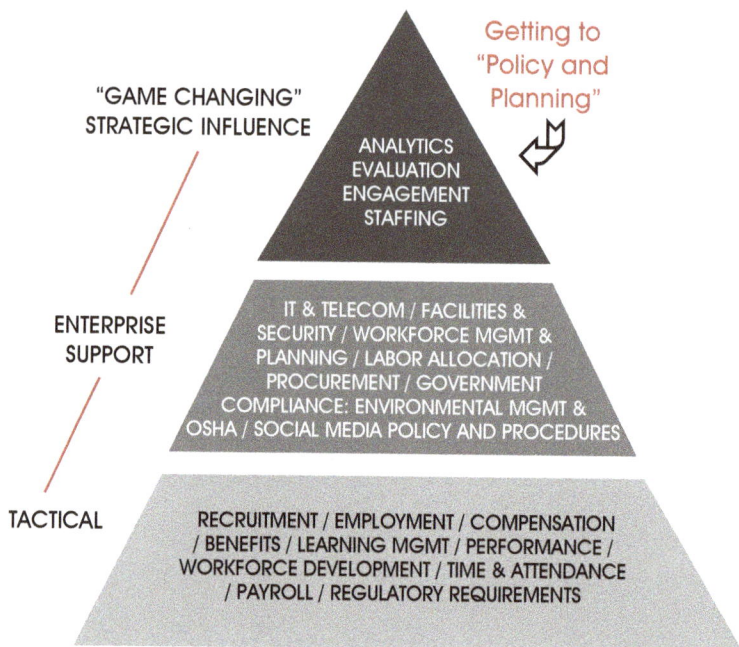

"GAME CHANGING" STRATEGIC INFLUENCE

Getting to "Policy and Planning"

ANALYTICS
EVALUATION
ENGAGEMENT
STAFFING

ENTERPRISE SUPPORT

IT & TELECOM / FACILITIES & SECURITY / WORKFORCE MGMT & PLANNING / LABOR ALLOCATION / PROCUREMENT / GOVERNMENT COMPLIANCE: ENVIRONMENTAL MGMT & OSHA / SOCIAL MEDIA POLICY AND PROCEDURES

TACTICAL

RECRUITMENT / EMPLOYMENT / COMPENSATION / BENEFITS / LEARNING MGMT / PERFORMANCE / WORKFORCE DEVELOPMENT / TIME & ATTENDANCE / PAYROLL / REGULATORY REQUIREMENTS

# How to gain the VALUE?

## HR must use the available HR Technology to create value by:

- ☐ Ensuring the availability of human capital by attracting, developing and retaining the best knowledge workers

- ☐ Reducing costs by providing operational effectiveness

- ☐ Aligning HR's mission/vision to help support and deliver the organizations' strategies

- ☐ Serving as a role model for reducing costs and achieving operational excellence

# HR must continue to evolve:

## What HR must focus on:
*(According to a SHRM poll of 4000 Senior HR Leaders – 2015)*

- ❐ Attracting and retaining a talented workforce;

- ❐ Developing leaders and establishing succession;

- ❐ Providing employees a self directed tool / application for "career enablement"; (see supporting materials Part 6/Section D)

- ❐ Providing support and tools for work group collaboration representing differing organizational components and staff;

- ❐ Supporting work group production from anywhere in the world, at any time.

# HR must strive to reduce ADMINISTRATION and increase its role in Policy and Planning

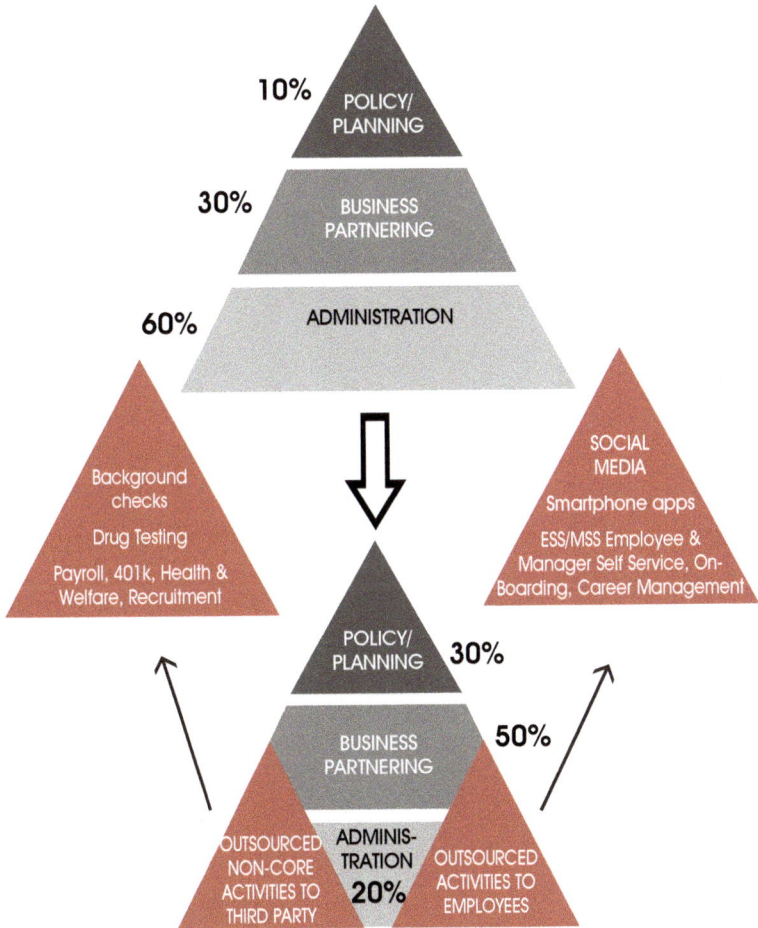

Note: Administration reduced from 60% to 20% through the use of Outsourcing, HR Technology delivered tools and functionality delivered over Cloud using self-service & social media.

# Now what?

As a professional in HR and using HR technology in some manner, what should you do? How do you manage your career to avoid being the target of others who seek to bypass you, or otherwise minimize your influence and thus, your **CLOUT?**

Here are two **"To-Do Lists"** that suggest activities for you to consider in order to enhance your personal CLOUT and to advance your career and put you into a position to increase your potential earnings:

# Your "TO-DO" List
## as an HR workforce member:

- ☐ **Know your company** and its' culture regarding employee growth and opportunity

- ☐ **Learn your industry** (competitors, trends)

- ☐ **Understand your "clients"** / stakeholders needs

- ☐ **Publicize** what the HR function does for your workforce - be proactive

- ☐ Participate in **industry benchmark** surveys

- ☐ Nurture informal relationships – **politic**

- ☐ Find a **mentor** – within your organization

- ☐ Review and **upgrade your job** description

- ☐ Remain current in **legislative trends**

- ☐ **Understand statistics, modeling**

- ☐ Know about the **other systems** in your company

- ☐ **Be visible**, publish, speak, teach, etc.

# Your TO-DO List
## as the caretaker of the HR technology environment - all of the previous, **plus**:

- ❐ Publicize your system AND your HR functions…be proactive

- ❐ Participate in industry benchmark surveys

- ❐ **Take the co-lead in any Workforce Cyber Awareness issues** (see Supporting Materials Part Six/Section C)

- ❐ Generate important metrics in a dashboard and distribute your findings and insights without waiting to be asked

- ❐ Seek bidirectional interfaces to other systems

- ❐ Know what your **industry cohorts** have and how they are using their HR technology – collaborate and share information.

# Importantly to those of us in HR:

**know your company** – along with self "introspection", listen to all **your** emotions and feelings . . . and **TRUST** them.

If you come to the realization that your organization is NOT providing you with new opportunities, new or ongoing training, internal career guidance, mentors, feedback more often than an annual formal Performance Evaluation, recognition, appropriate rewards, and a feeling of alignment and belonging into the workplace culture, then your next move will become obvious to you.

# Know your company!
## – it's critically important

❑ **Take control of your career,** don't be passive, don't wait for management to provide you with opportunities, although it is great when they do, but seize the initiative, **do not let yourself be perceived as an obstacle and become targeted as Ms. H.R. Job was.**


❑ **Be a willing collaborator**, if not an innovator, possessing a positive mindset and abilities to share all with your colleagues.

Recognize that the foundation for your success and your ability to gain CLOUT and influence originates with your access to, and how you use, DATA.

So remember that . . .

- ❏ Data should lead to **information**

- ❏ Information could lead to **influence**

- ❏ Influence should lead to **power**

- ❏ Power and influence means **CLOUT**

- ❏ **CLOUT should lead to NEW programs leading to personal and professional success!**

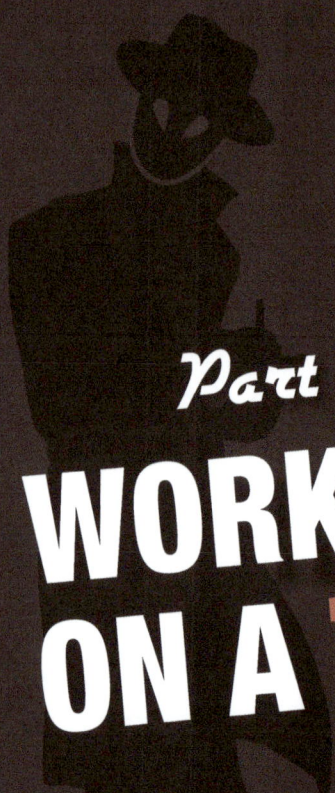

*Part Four:*

# WORKING ON A TEAM

AND PRESERVING YOUR
SPHERE OF **INFLUENCE**
AND **CLOUT**

# *Contents:*

Lessons from an alien species who visit Earth in 1951's Sci-fi classic:

"THE DAY THE EARTH STOOD STILL"

So now you might have some
POWER & INFLUENCE, ie. **CLOUT**.

But, sharing your influence and
using it to collaborate with others is
not easy.

Do you know how to use it when
working with others on teams
throughout the globe . . .
**and beyond?**

Working with others, from all other backgrounds, cultures and ideals is NEVER EASY, BECAUSE . . .

Technology Projects Fail or Succeed **NOT** because of Software or Technology **BUT** because of the way **PEOPLE (on TEAMS, or as individuals) Behave and COMMUNICATE!**

# Why do projects fail?

❑ Politics

❑ Management philosophy
  not in alignment with the
  company itself

❑ Unclear, missing, and poorly
  communicated goals,
  vision and objectives

❑ Team dysfunctions

❑ Human interactions:
  – people to people –
  virtual and face to face

**CONFLICT IS A PROBLEM THAT
HAS EXISTED FOR AS LONG
AS PEOPLE INHABITED THE
EARTH!**

# Who are the people
## whose conflicts can cause problems?

☐ End Users/Subject Matter Experts (SME) and Systems People

☐ Vendor Representatives and Clients or Prospects

☐ Department Staff - HR and IT, HR and Finance, HR and other departments

☐ Managers and Team members reporting to them

☐ Men and Women!

**AND EVEN BETWEEN HUMANS AND ALIENS!**

One message that resonates with this author to this day, is the lessons emanating from the classic Sci-Fi movie "The Day the Earth Stood Still." Over the years I have used clips from that movie with my own voice-over to make the point about human bias, perceptions and first impressions and the challenges of communications among people on projects.

Take a look ⟶

In the 1951 movie, *The Day the Earth Stood Still*, a humanoid alien visitor named **Klaatu** comes to Earth accompanied by an 8 foot robot, **GORT**, to deliver an important message that will affect the entire human race.

Landing of saucer  ⟶

## The Alien emerges –
## offering a gift and is shot

When a flying saucer lands in Washington D.C.
the Army quickly surrounds it. A humanoid **(Mr.
Klaatu)** emerges announcing that "**he has come in
peace**." He is shot by a nervous soldier. A tall robot
emerges from the saucer and quickly disintegrates
the soldiers' weapons. The alien orders the robot
**GORT** to stop. He explains that the now broken
device "is a gift for your President, with this he would
be able to study **"life on other ~~planets~~."** projects

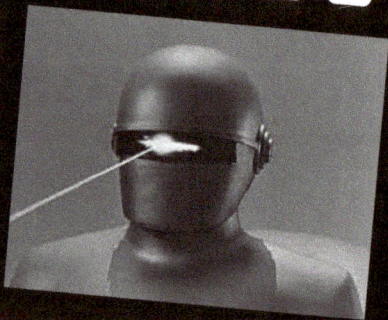

Take Me To Your Leader

# "We Come In Peace, To Serve"

"Communication - the human connection - is the key to personal and career success."

- Paul J. Meyer, author of *The 5 Pillars of Leadership*

We must understand the Laws of the Galaxy . . . the Laws of Communications, or ELSE!

**The ALIEN is visited by the Secretary to the President in the hospital after being shot.**

**Klaatu** is visited by the President's secretary, Mr. Harley who asks him "where he is from" – **Klaatu** says "from another Planet Department. **Klaatu** tells him that he has a message that must be delivered to all the world's leaders simultaneously. Harley states that would be impossible. He looks puzzled. **Klaatu** later escapes, and demonstrates his power by stopping all electricity in the world for 30 minutes (except at hospitals).

**The Secretary looks puzzled. He just doesn't get it. . .**

## "GET" WHAT?

The film shows us that inherent personal beliefs, pre-dispositions, fear, rush to judgment, and poor training can all lead to dysfunction and poor outcomes for any team effort.

All Technology projects involve teamwork – especially an HR project needing input from multiple functional representatives who themselves have many varying experiences, along with their own set of "issues" within the company and their own career.

These projects can be improved, conflicts can be avoided, and team collaboration can have a greater chance of success by understanding each individual's;

- ❑ Behavior and Motivation

- ❑ Communication Style

- ❑ Conflict Resolution and Decision Making Style

- ❑ Team Participation Style

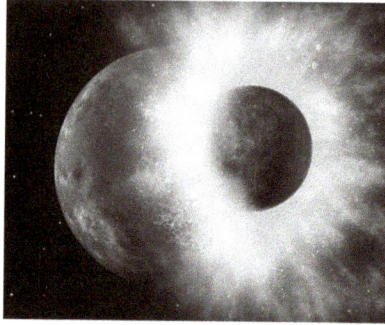

# When Worlds Collide!

Individuals and Teams react according to:

- ❑ their **"own interests"**

- ❑ their **"thirst for power"**

If INTERESTS and DEGREE OF THIRST FOR POWER are NOT ALIGNED with others on the TEAM/PROJECT, interactions will lead to **CONFLICT**.

# When Worlds Collide!

## *Why Conflicts Exist*

Individuals react to other individuals based on many factors that differ between them:

- ❏ Goals
- ❏ Information
- ❏ Methods
- ❏ Feelings
- ❏ Personality
- ❏ Values and Beliefs
- ❏ Perceptions
- ❏ Fears
- ❏ Agendas
- ❏ Experience

AND . . . ➡

# When Worlds Collide!

## Why Conflicts Exist

... are influenced by the Organization itself
*AND*

... Organizational **"politics"**

- ❑ **Conflicts** arise whenever Interests collide

- ❑ Collisions create stress and tension, which create **"Politics"** and **Resistance to Change**

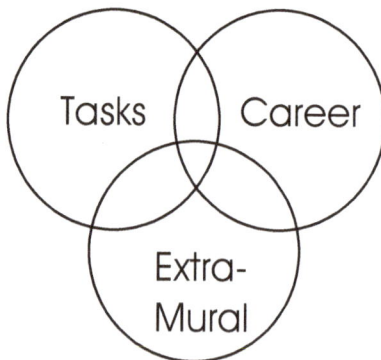

# When Worlds Collide!

*Within any organization there are many opportunities for conflict to arise between supervisors, peers and subordinates:*

**YOUR SELF-PERCEIVED ROLE AND EXPECTATIONS VERSUS THOSE OF OTHERS**

⇔ **organizational** role, responsibilities

⇔ **your** off the job and life roles

⇔ your **supervisors** self-perceived role/expectations..

⇔ your supervisor's expectation of **your** role

⇔ **your** expectations and perceptions of your supervisor's role

⇔ your **subordinates** expectations and perceptions of your role

⇔ your **subordinates** self-perceived role/expectation

⇔ your **peers** self perceived role/ expectation

⇔ your **peers** expectation of your role

⇔ your expectations of **your peers** role/expectation

# When Worlds Collide!

## *Why Individuals Resist Change*

- ❑ Impact on Self

- ❑ Fear of Unknown

- ❑ Sense of Anxiety

- ❑ Uncertainty

- ❑ Loss of Values

- ❑ Loss of personal **POWER or CLOUT**

# When Worlds Collide!

**Everyone wants some kind of POWER. Those that already have power are afraid of losing it. Here are the typical types of POWER:**

**Reward Power:** doing a task to get something of perceived value. Reward power can also be used to increase morale. Think of giving a trophy to the highest performer or the team with the lowest amount of mistakes. This type of reward can become a highly sought-after status symbol within your organization.

**Coercive power:** forcing someone to do something against their will or setting up "consequences" to employee actions.

**Legitimate power:** is the power of position or role. This is the typical "command and control" structure that is employed by the Military world. Legitimate Power acts as a formalized way of ensuring that there is someone to make a decision (good or bad) and that someone is responsible.

**Informational Power:** of having information that another does not have, or, the distribution of information as a means of effecting change. This could be positive or negative propaganda, knowledge of an opponents strategy, or detailed information that is used in decision support.

# When Worlds Collide!

## Types of Power *(continued)*:

**Expert power:** Closely related to Informational Power, Expert Power is when an individual possesses in-depth information, knowledge, or expertise in the area that they are responsible for. This type of power is often the most effective type of power. This is the CHRO, or the Software Architect, the lead engineer, the CFO, CTO, a MD, or PhD, or other highly skilled and highly trained employee.

**Referent power:** is the "cult of personality." This is the power and ability for an individual to attract others and to build loyalty within them. Referent Power is also the power of respect. This can occur through time if a leader is successful and has a well known track-record of success. Referent Power is also created through the values of the individual.

**Connection power:** is gained by a person knowing another person who has the power and networks successfully and gains influence by being in an "inner circle". Also called "knowing the Gatekeeper well."

# When Worlds Collide!

In your role (and its responsibilities) in HR or anywhere else **YOU** must recognize **WHO** in the organization has the Power, Influence and CLOUT (besides yourself).

It would be the people who have:

- ❑ **Formal Authority**
- ❑ Control of **Scarce Resources**
- ❑ Control of **Decision Processes**
- ❑ Control of **Knowledge and Information**
- ❑ Control of the **Dissemination of Knowledge**
- ❑ **Control of Technology**
- ❑ **Interpersonal Alliances, Networks**
- ❑ Control of the **"Informal Organization"**

# When Worlds Collide!

Sometimes people of influence are very different from us, especially if they seem from another world! And thus have an **Alien Brain.**

How Are **They** Different From **Us**?

# When Worlds Collide!

## *Alien Brains*

## Team person 1: from **HR**

Typically or stereotyped as:

- ❑ Outgoing-"people person"
- ❑ Used to long, unstructured projects
- ❑ Right brained
- ❑ Not used to fast feedback
- ❑ Not early to adapt high tech solutions
- ❑ Qualitative/subjective
- ❑ Not a fan of spreadsheets

# When Worlds Collide!

## Alien Brains

## Team person 2: **a Payroll person**

Typically or stereotyped as:

- ❑ At times outgoing
  (only after a successful Payroll run)
- ❑ "Left brained"
- ❑ Used to immediate feedback
- ❑ Desires low visibility in an
  organization
- ❑ Quantitative, loves Government
  forms
- ❑ Not normally a "fashion plate"

# When Worlds Collide!

## *Alien Brains*

## Team person 3: **somebody from SYSTEMS/"IT"**

Typically or stereotyped as:

- ❑ "Nerdy" "Geeky"
- ❑ Gadgets galore, early adaptors
- ❑ Precise and Quantitative
- ❑ At times lacking social graces
- ❑ Uncomfortable in one-on-one interactions
- ❑ Independent contributor
- ❑ Socializes mostly with other IT types

# When Worlds Collide!

## *Alien Brains*

## Team person 4: **Vendor People**

Typically or stereotyped as:

- ❏ Aggressive
- ❏ Well Paid
- ❏ Personable and Friendly
- ❏ Focused
- ❏ Well Educated
- ❏ Customer Service Driven

# When Worlds Collide!

## *Power to the Species!*
## *. . . . Getting along!*

The Species: HR, Benefits, Payroll, Systems & Vendors (Humans all)

- ❏ The **POWER** Problem:
  Everyone Wants It!

- ❏ The **POWER** Solution:
  we must FIRST understand each
  other and then **Share/Collaborate**
  to harness and utilize **POWER**
  collectively!

# Peace in Our Galaxy:

## *Conflict Resolution*

Returning to the lessons from the movie **"The Day the Earth Stood Still,"** **Klaatu** escapes and travels to the home of a respected scientist along with his new friend. While enroute, **Klaatu** says "I'm worried about **GORT**." She responds, "but he is a robot." He states, "unleashed he can destroy the Earth" and adds "should anything happen to me, she must say to **GORT**, 'Klaatu, Barada, Nikto.'"

# Peace in Our Galaxy:

*Conflict Resolution*

Later, the woman is cornered and threatened by the robot **GORT** and defuses his intent by saying what she was told to say:

"**GORT** – Klaatu, Berada, Nikto; Klaatu, Berada, Nikto"

# Peace in Our Galaxy:

## *Conflict Resolution – Miller's Alien language definitions*

What I suggest the words mean:

**KLAATU** ⟶ Preserve Dignity and Self Respect by Listening with Empathy

**BERADA** ⟶ Don't expect to change what others are

**NIKTO** ⟶ Share, don't shout your independent perspective

# Peace in Our Galaxy:

## *Team Building*

To be **effective**, a Team must have a foundation of these characteristics:

- ❑ Clear Purpose and Goals
- ❑ Informality
- ❑ Participation of all
- ❑ Mutual respect among all
- ❑ **Civilized** Disagreement
- ❑ Consensus Decisions
- ❑ Spirited and enjoyable attitudes and outreach

# Peace in Our Galaxy:

## *Team Building*

Successful Team building strategies for Team Leaders:

- ☐ Get to know the Team as **Individuals**
- ☐ Define the Team's purpose
- ☐ Jointly, develop the Project Plan and targets
- ☐ Clarify roles, establish norms, encourage feedback and participation
- ☐ Share the limelight
- ☐ Celebrate accomplishments, **have fun!**
- ☐ Assess Team effectiveness

# Peace in Our Galaxy:

## *Team Building*

So, you can think you are the **Center of the Universe** . . .

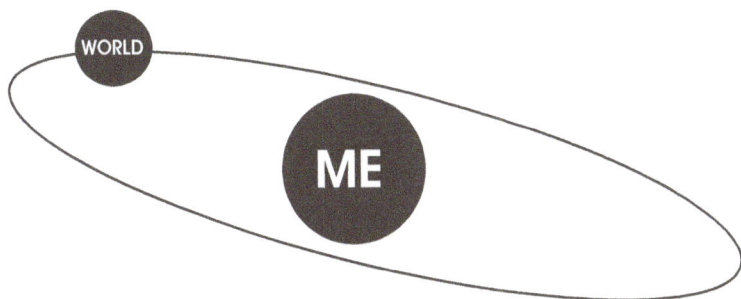

or, you can approach your dealings with others ("species") as being part of a bigger Universe, as **Klaatu** suggests.

Don't take stuff so seriously, remember...

You are here.

# A Parting Message:

*Getting Along with Anyone, Anywhere, No Matter What "Universe" they operate in . . .*

The original movie dialogue is transcribed on the next page.

Once again the words shown in RED are my voice-over replacements when the movie clip is shown during my talks on the topic of **CLOUT** and team dynamics.

**Klaatu** emerges from the saucer and addresses the World's assembled scientists, informing them that he represents an "interplanetary organization that created a police force of invincible robots like **GORT** to patrol the planets in spaceships like this one, and preserve the peace" by automatically annihilating aggressors. "In matters of aggression, we have given them absolute power over us. This power cannot be revoked." **Klaatu** concludes with, "It is no concern of ours how you run your own ~~planet~~, PROJECT but if you threaten to extend your violence, this ~~Earth~~ COMPANY of yours will be reduced to a burned-out cinder. **Your choice is simple: join us and live in peace, or pursue your present course and face obliteration.**"

**Klaatu** ends his message to the Earth's people with

"THE DECISION RESTS WITH YOU!"

**Klaatu** and **GORT** re-enter the spaceship and depart.

# Back to our crime

Ms. H.R. Job was unable to internalize the fact that she herself was an obstacle to progress.

She did not realize that her work attitude was perceived as an **obstacle** by others in her organization.

She seemed not to face, nor consider the many decisions she was faced with – relating to how she continued her tasks in her changing work environment.

She certainly seemed unaware of how much her work environment was changing and what that change meant to her activities and to her attitude.

# Part Five:

# STAYING

# VIGILANT

ANTICIPATING WHAT
IS LIKELY TO CHANGE IN
THE NEXT FEW YEARS

# Contents:

KEEPING YOUR **CLOUT** IN THE AGE OF **ARTIFICIAL INTELLIGENCE (AI)** IN HUMAN RESOURCES ADMINISTRATION.

- ❏ IS **AI** AN HRJob KILLER?
  OR IS **AI** AN IMPORTANT TEAMMATE
  AND COLLABORATOR?

- ❏ THE IMPACT OF **AI** ON THE ROLE
  AND RESPONSIBILITIES WITHIN THE
  REALM OF HUMAN RESOURCES

# The new transformation in Mindset;

**From GORT** – a robot to be feared, to the strong probability of a future requiring collaboration between humans and robots in the workforce.

As the original movie **"The Day the Earth Stood Still"** (released in 1951 by 20th Century Fox) proved popular, it was widely perceived as a **"Statement Film"** written and produced by Hollywood to bring awareness to the dangerous conduct of humankind's Nuclear testing and the resultant increase of Cold War tensions and the ever more likelihood of global destruction.

Similarly, the emergence of **AI** has prompted much talk about the impact of ROBOTS on all of the global workforce as the year 2020 approaches. **Part Five discusses this as a direct impact on the role, if not survival of Ms. H. R. Job.**

# The future impact of **Artificial Intelligence** on the Role and even survival of HRJob (the person and the function).

❑ As we have seen, "Mr. Arturo Intelligente" was, of course, under early consideration as a prime suspect in the crime of ending Ms. H.R. Job's career (and life).

❑ **Artificial Intelligence** must be embraced in a way that serves the organization to the best possible extent. HRJob among all other impacted functions must either co-exist or fade away.

❑ How everyone reacts to this threat to the very existence of HRJob and its responsibilities will be seen in the next few years.

❑ The following shows the extent of the impact of **AI** on HR and some important observations of senior leaders . . .

# Your replacement?
# Or your Teammate?

The impact of **AI** on the role and responsibilities within the realm of Human Resources

# INTRODUCTION:

- ❏ No doubt about it, **AI** will impact all industries and a good many roles within the workplace.
- ❏ According to the HCI (Human Capital Institute):
  - ◆ By 2020 75% of organizations will implement **AI** projects.
  - ◆ By 2023 **AI** will be as smart as a person.
  - ◆ By 2045 **AI** will be smarter than all brains combined on earth.
  - ◆ **AI** technologies that can automate processes and increase team capacity are here:
    - ▪ **JP Morgan** developed an **AI** solution that saved 360,000 hours of work annually previously performed by attorneys in less than 3 years.
    - ▪ **Lowe's** is rolling out robots that assist shoppers and scan inventory levels.
    - ▪ **Amtrak's** customer service bot increased bookings by 25% at a savings of $1M annually.

# INTRODUCTION *(continued)*

❑ **AI** is a machine's ability to mimic human capabilities such as learning, problem solving, and perception. For HR, this is the application of artificial intelligence to the function in order to streamline or automate some part of the workflow.

❑ It is my belief that any position in HR - held by any generation of worker – must not fear **AI**, must NOT think of **AI** as a threat, must not expect to be working **for** a robot. On the contrary, HRJob must think of Artificial Intelligence – not as embodied by Mr. Arturo Intelligente (in our Crime Scene investigation) but as a **helpful collaborator!**

❑ **I am not alone in voicing this approach, and I would hope that my readers consider the inevitability and benefits of AI as discussed on the following pages by industry leaders.**

# Artificial Intelligence:
## What is it?, What can **AI** do?

❑ "Artificial intelligence" is a term that is almost as misunderstood as "human resources." HR and **AI** have both been hyped as strategic assets that will change the future of work, but the reality of these promises never seems to arrive. Over the next three to ten years that may finally change.

❑ **Artificial intelligence** — most specifically a combination of machine learning and natural language processing — has matured to the point that it is practically useful in a workplace setting. Anyone who has ever asked aloud for Siri, Alexa, Cortana, or Google to search the internet, schedule an appointment, or order a book — and had their smart device fulfill the order — understands what this technology is already capable of.

❑ Modern **AI** software can understand written and spoken language far better than ever before, and **AI** can use that understanding to take action. Over the next three to five years, this technology will be applied to a number of common, repetitive administrative functions — many of which are normally conducted by HR staff.

# Artificial Intelligence:
## What is it?, What can **AI** do?

❑ If IBM's "Watson" could (and can, and did!) ingest and analyze the entire Wikipedia and use it to answer Jeopardy! questions, the same principle could be used to scan the entirety of your employee insurance policies to answer common questions during your annual open enrollment period. Similarly, employee handbooks and training guides can be turned into self-updating FAQ documents with little to no direct human oversight.

❑ Automating these tedious, commodity tasks will free up HR to finally start fulfilling its role as a strategic advisor to the organization. Importantly though, HR will have to be more selective about whom it hires to oversee the desired and needed strategic role within the remaining HR functions. **This, however, is just the beginning of AI's potential role in Human Resources.**

# Artificial Intelligence:
## What is it?, What can **AI** do?

❑ Over the next 10 years, artificial intelligence
will create the analytics suite that will empower
HR to become a truly metrics-driven aspect of
your company. Email has been in common
use for 20 years, instant messaging and
social media for 10, and chat platforms like
Slack have just gone mainstream — and all
of them consist of millions or even billions of
unstructured employee communications. AI
will eventually read and analyze these silos of
information to proactively determine which
common questions need answering, which
common complaints need to be addressed,
and which common tasks need a new full
time employee to oversee.

# Artificial Intelligence:
## What is it?, What can **AI** do?

❑ **AI**-empowered sentiment analysis will go
further, offering HR an "emotional dashboard"
for their organization. Human Resources staff
will spot burnout from common cues and
intervene before it becomes problematic.
Passive HR managers and other managers
who guide projects and processes along
throughout an organization without obvious
notice will be spotted by algorithms and
earmarked for needed training, job
enrichment and eventually, promotion or
other kinds of career enablement. The true
state of employee satisfaction — and the
management communication triggers that
actually affect morale — will be qualitatively
evaluated to create actionable insights.

# Artificial Intelligence:
## What is it?, What can **AI** do?

❑ Artificial intelligence is on the verge of turning all employee communications into data, and all communications patterns into automated processes. "Bots" will answer common questions, complete common forms, and free Human Resources from administrative drudgery. Freed from the burden of insurance enrollments and annual review proctoring, HR will have the time to strategically advise the organization. **Empowered with AI analytics, Human Resources will be able to use that time to fine-tune the performance of the actual humans in the workforce, and drive companies to new heights of employee productivity and engagement.**

# Artificial Intelligence:
## What is it?, What can **AI** do?

- ❑ **A recent survey found that 38% of enterprises are already using AI in their workplace with 62% expecting to use it by 2018. According to Josh Bersin at Deloitte, 33% of employees expect their jobs will become augmented by AI in the near future.**

- ❑ To understand the impact of **AI** on HR, a survey of HR executives by IBM found that 46% believe **AI** will transform their talent acquisition capability and 49% believe it will transform their payroll and benefits administration.

# The Impact of **AI** on the Role and Responsibilities within the Realm of Human Resources

An ongoing debate is whether **AI** will replace HR in the workplace. **Here are 10 HR leaders who believe AI technology will support, rather than replace HR.**

Thank you to Ms. JI-A MIN – head scientist at Ideal whose article appears in *Personnel Today newsletter* – April 26, 2017.

1. **AI will automate screening and reduce bias** -Somen Mondal, CEO of IDEAL SOFTWARE – software that uses **AI** to automate recruiting tasks, believes **AI's** biggest impact will be in automating candidate screening and reducing bias.

   - ❏ **AI** can learn the qualifications of employees who are successful in a role and apply this knowledge to screen, rank, and grade candidates who match the criteria.

   - ❏ According to Mondal, companies using **AI** for recruiting software have seen promising results such as a 71% decrease in cost per hire and a threefold increase in recruiter efficiency.

   - ❏ Mondal is also excited by **AI's** potential to reduce unconscious bias during the screening process, since **AI** can ignore demographic-related information about a candidate's age, race, and sex.

# The Impact of **AI** on the Role and Responsibilities within the Realm of Human Resources

## 2. AI will reduce errors and improve compliance

❏ Joey Price, CEO of Jumpstart: HR – a managed HR services provider, thinks **AI** will help reduce errors and minimize compliance fines.

❏ Because he believes **AI** is best suited for collecting and compiling data quickly and without human error, Price predicts mid- to senior-level professionals will reap the value of **AI** the most.

## 3. AI will augment corporate training

❏ Simon Rakosi, co-founder of Butterfly – a real-time leadership coaching platform, thinks the biggest impact **AI** will have on HR is augmenting corporate training and coaching.

❏ He views coaching via **AI** as a way to help managers understand their team's feedback and put it to use immediately.

❏ While **AI** can replace the delegation aspect of management, **Rakosi believes true leaders can't be replaced because AI won't be able to replace soft skills that empower, motivate and develop employees.**

# The Impact of **AI** on the Role and Responsibilities within the Realm of Human Resources

## 4. AI will increase adoption of metrics and analytics

- ❏ Ira S. Wolfe, President of Success Performance Solutions – a recruitment consultancy, states **AI** will help HR finally become a strategic partner through the adoption of metrics and analytics.

- ❏ Using analytics, Wolfe believes **AI** will help managers identify new hires with the highest probability of success, place them on the right teams paired with the right supervisor, recommend learning opportunities and career path options, and even suggest the likelihood of their flight risk.

## 5. AI will enhance candidate assessment

- ❏ Erica Hill, managing editor at HireVue – software that combines digital video with predictive analytics, is excited by **AI's** potential to enhance recruiters' ability to make hiring decisions.

- ❏ She believes **AI** can help assess candidates and speed up time to hire without sacrificing quality of hire. For example, **AI can turn a 15-minute video interview into a set of 20,000 data points on facial movements, intonation, and word choice to assess a candidate.**

# The Impact of **AI** on the Role and Responsibilities within the Realm of Human Resources

## 6. AI will automate candidate outreach

❑ Aaron Prebluda, CMO at KUNUNU USA – a talent community that features company reviews, believes **AI** will enable us to be more productive and efficient by automating tasks.

❑ In terms of recruiting and managing talent, Prebluda sees the areas where **AI** will have the biggest impact as CV screening, interview scheduling, and communication with candidates.

❑ He argues, however, that automating tasks does not reduce the need for people. Instead, **AI** automation creates more time for people to tackle bigger, more important challenges.

## 7. AI will streamline employee onboarding

❑ Adelyn Zhou, chief marketing officer of TOPBOTS – an **AI** research, education and advisory firm, positions **AI's** role as replacing many of the mundane tasks in HR and freeing HR's time to focus on what they do best: nurturing, cultivating, and working with talent.

❑ She predicts intelligent bots will act as virtual assistants in the employee onboarding process, by creating new employee profiles and helping staff answer basic questions about benefits, insurance, and company policies.

# The Impact of **AI** on the Role and Responsibilities within the Realm of Human Resources

## 8. AI will improve workplace learning

❑ George Elfond, CEO at Rallyware – a workforce engagement platform, states the use of **AI** in HR is still getting to the point of critical mass of data. He believes the quicker that companies embrace AI technologies, the easier it will be for them to adapt and lead in the future.

❑ According to Elfond, **companies who have employed AI-based learning technology have seen impressive results, such as a 32% increase in employee productivity and a 43% increase in employee retention.**

## 9. AI will reveal new insights on talent

❑ Alicia Shankland, Principal at Huntbridge – an executive search and consulting firm, is excited by AI's potential to challenge long-held HR assumptions with new insights.

❑ Shankland envisions **AI** will give us insights that can open up entirely new candidate pools by identifying a diverse set of experiences, abilities, and mindsets that are better predictors of success.

# The Impact of **AI** on the Role and Responsibilities within the Realm of Human Resources

## 10. AI will show the value of the human touch

- ❑ Steve Pritchard, HR Consultant for Ben Sherman – a UK menswear brand, touts **AI** as an exciting advancement that promises to make day-to-day life for HR much easier.

- ❑ He predicts that while artificial intelligence will be beneficial for HR in terms of helping with record keeping and dealing with tasks that can be automated, it will never replace people.

- ❑ Pritchard believes no amount of technology can replace the simple comfort and reassurance that comes from **speaking to another human being who cares.**

So, it seems that many thoughtful executives are of the impression that HR should not be in fear of AI, nor consider it a threat to the existence of the overall function.

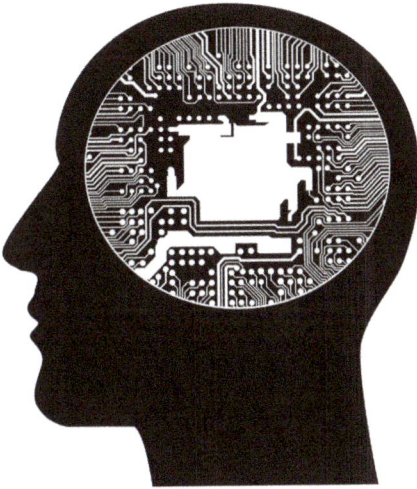

# AI and HR

It is hoped that being a Teammate and not a "Job Killer" – will be the eventual adaptation of **AI** and its affect on the function of Human Resources.

And, it is not unreasonable that in the near term of just a few years, a humanoid robot of the future will do most, if not all of the very specific administrative workflow – requiring no intuitive skills. **Skills that Ms. Harriet Rose Job was an expert in, much to her misfortune!**

HOWEVER, intuitiveness is already a strong capability of many of the robots already being used in leading edge companies as you are reading this.

# So, remember the opening quote from Ms. Ginni Rometty CEO at IBM...

IBM'S WATSON will only be a cause for concern, if you fail to embrace the possibilities, and fail to grab the wave of change.

As stated by Ms. Rometty, **Define yourself, Don't let anyone else define you.** Seek to be a "colleague" of "Watson" or any other **AI** algorithms you come into contact with.

HR folks, seek more responsibility. Take more initiative. Do what it takes to add to your influence and use your **CLOUT**.

Seek to embrace **AI.** By working with **AI**, YOU will improve the role and responsibilities of all staff, at all levels within the function of Human Resources to the overall benefit of your organization.

Returning to our crime once again, the question of WHO KILLED H. (Harriet) R. (Rose) Job?

## Final Thoughts

### WHO DID IT?

It could have been **any one of the "Suspects" and other "Persons of Interest."** I chose to select just a few.

### WHY DID IT HAPPEN?

Ms. Harriet Rose Job, by her own work practices and attitude, gave motive to all the members of her organization. The work landscape itself was a big motivator as well. By her being perceived as an unneeded **obstacle** to a variety of progressive initiatives with the corporation, Ms. H. R. Job made herself an easy target for elimination.

## HOW DO YOU AVOID MS. H. R. JOB'S FATE?

Readers, you have a great opportunity to leverage technology to generate strategic valued information, grasp new roles and lead even more progressive initiatives in your organization, even to the extent that you collaborate with or embrace Artificial Intelligence.

Take charge of your own career and make sure you work for an organization that has a culture of career enablement, properly rewards all its workforce and has exhibited a clear message, with supportive actions (and with budget support) **that show a belief in the strategic value of Human Resources in a business partner role.**

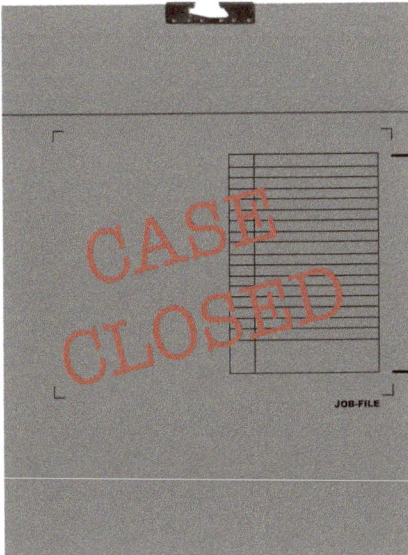

# Part Six:

# SUPPORTING
# MATERIALS

# Contents:

**A.** A suggested beginning of an effective HRJob "mission statement".

**B.** Specific details on a variety of important Metrics that are desirable to senior management for strategic decision making purposes.

**C.** A suggested new initiative to be seized by HRJob as a co-leader along with IT/Security executives in owning and delivering the message of **awareness of Cybersecurity threats to the entire workforce.**

**D.** A brief discussion of **new HR software providers** whose functionality builds CLOUT and supports, at the employee level, career management / advancement and thus places the responsibility of delivering those initiatives within the scope of **HRJob.**

# Introduction:

❑ As the role of HRJob remains under pressure from the forces of **Artificial Intelligence**, vendors taking advantage of built-in logarithms and bots, higher expectations of executives expecting a nimble and already identified expert workforce ready for any assignment anywhere in the world, **HRJob must seize issues and initiatives that come their way in order to stay relevant and value adding.**

❑ **HRJob – as we have seen, must not remain passive and satisfied with performing tasks that add no proven value and which add nothing to their reputation.**

❑ The material presented herein is intended to provide some foundation and content for which HRJob, at any level, can build upon for the purpose of increasing their functions' visibility and the influence, power and thus **CLOUT** of the HR professional.

❑ If Ms. H. (Harriet) R. (Rose) Job had embraced any of the initiatives presented herein, it is quite reasonable to speculate that she would be alive and thriving.

# Introduction (cont'd):

❏ Maybe just one series of metrics presented as a dashboard would have been enough to ensure her survival? Or maybe, taking the lead on finding a third party to train her organization's workforce on Cybersecurity threats, or maybe seeking a new and up-and-coming HR Technology vendor to help herself and her workforce gain a new path to the positions they knowingly or unknowingly desire, would have ensured her survival.

❏ Taking any initiative, any at all, can be seen as adding value to an organization. It could be life saving!

# A. HR MISSION STATEMENT

# A. HR MISSION STATEMENT

## A mission statement for HR initiatives and more…

HRJob needs to be aware and work towards supporting all aspects of this (suggested) mission statement.

- ❑ "To radically improve the value, effectiveness and cost structure of HR, through the use of technologically rich solutions that fundamentally alter the way HR provides strategic advice, expertise and administrative services to employees and managers."

- ❑ "HR must be the proprietor of services to the entire workforce that enables, and thus engages, each individual within the workforce no matter their role or responsibilities, in managing their own career progression by providing all necessary opportunities for self enrichment and advancement."

# B. HR METRICS & DASHBOARDS

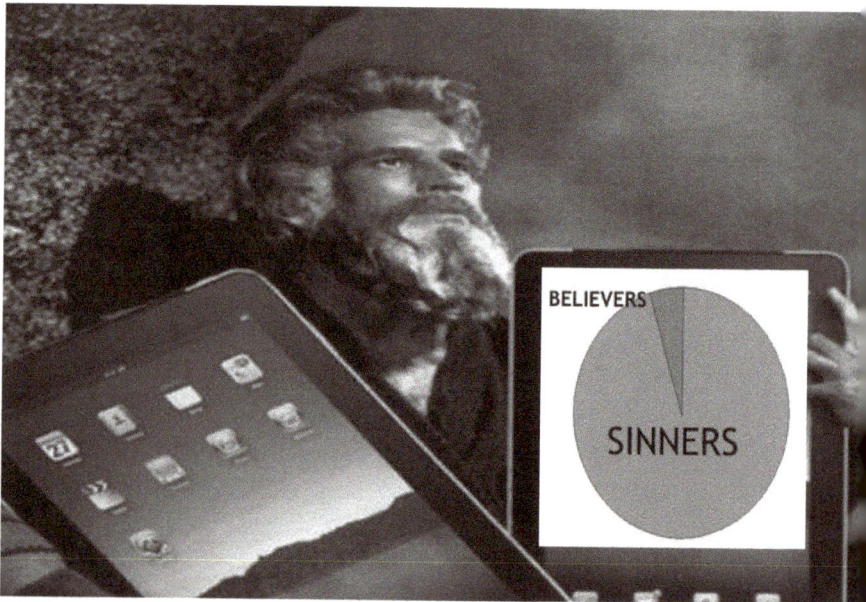

Metrics have been around a long time!

# B. HR METRICS AND DASHBOARDS

## The Importance of Metrics

❑ Metrics are the representation of data in a form that shows either a static situation or the direction of the effects of a specific program or activity (such as turnover). The static form of metrics show exactly that, a static, point in time, current level of a calculated depiction of levels of workforce, costs, revenue, sales, skills, etc. **This data is important to those that need it, but "point-in-time reports are usually not strategic or value adding.**

❑ **Metrics that show future trends over time, combined with other parameters are likely to be considered more value-adding to the top decision makers**. Combined and displayed graphically, and pleasing to the eye, and easily absorbed by leadership, metrics, now called Workforce Analytics, are a critical outcome of the underlying data routinely maintained in a well developed HR technology delivery: a system of integrated HR/Payroll/Benefits functionality or one that focuses on a specific HR function, such as Talent Management.

❑ Importantly and more recently, metrics based upon an underlying pattern of individual workforce behaviors and attitudes, along with the inclusion of algorithms and insights (similar to those used in **AI**) that are based on thousands of points of data are now presented as **"Predictive Analytics."**

❑ Some HRMS providers already use this approach, although limited, in delivering reports regarding Workforce Talent such as the **"Nine-box" model**, which shows potential tendencies for top performing employees to exit, even before they know that they want to.

❑ It is reasonable to suggest that if Ms. Harriet Rose Job had taken the initiative, asked senior management what metrics they would like or need, and generated a "trial balloon" of a dashboard report, it might have saved her from her fate.

# B. HR METRICS AND DASHBOARDS

# B. HR METRICS AND DASHBOARDS

## HR Performance Dashboard

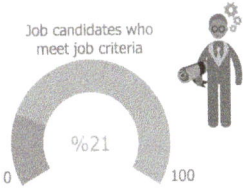

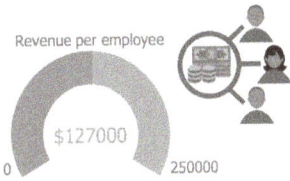

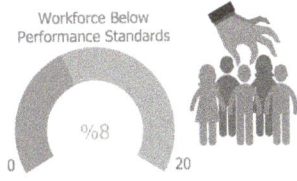

Job candidates who meet job criteria

%21

0 — 100

Monthly internal hire rate

%4

0 — 20

Revenue per employee

$127000

0 — 250000

Workforce Below Performance Standards

%8

0 — 20

# B. HR METRICS AND DASHBOARDS

**Here are some common Human Capital oriented Metrics showing the ROI of the "human asset" for an organization.**

Human Capital Revenue Factor (HCRF)

> – Total Revenue / Full Time Equivalent (FTE)

Human Economic Value Added (HEVA)

> – (Net Operating Margin – Cost of Capital) / Full Time Equivalent (FTE)

Human Capital Cost Factor (HCCF)

> –W2 Pay + Cost of Contingent Labor + Cost of Absenteeism + Cost of Turnover

Human Capital Value Added (HCVA)

> –Operating Revenue – (Operating Expenses – Pay and Benefits) / FTEs

Human Capital Return on Investment (HCROI)

> –Operating Revenue – (Operating Expenses – Pay and Benefits) / Pay and Benefits

# B. HR METRICS AND DASHBOARDS

This list originated with **Saratoga Institute (now part of PWC).** It is one of the first listings of valuable HR metrics and is a good starting point for socializing early metrics reporting to senior level management: (details of each calculation can be found on the PWC / Saratoga website.

- ❑ Benefit Factor (% of total salary)
- ❑ Cost per Hire
- ❑ Employee Cost Factor
- ❑ Human Capital ROI
- ❑ HR Headcount Ratio
- ❑ Income Factor
- ❑ Management Ratio
- ❑ Revenue Factor
- ❑ Training Cost Factor
- ❑ Voluntary Separation Rate

# B. HR METRICS AND DASHBOARDS

Here are some "pure" Human Resources metrics that can be provided in some form or another (preferably graphically) to HR's "stakeholders"

|  | Expressed As | Computed As |
|---|---|---|
| Work Force Productivity | Net income/ee | $\dfrac{\text{Net income}}{\text{Total Active Employees}}$ |
|  | Production Output (per employee) | $\dfrac{\text{\#Units Output/ Hourly Employee}}{\text{Total Hourly Active Employees}}$ |
|  | Dollars of Sales (per employee) | $\dfrac{\text{Dollars Value or Units Sold}}{\text{Total \# of Active Employees}}$ |
| Compensation | Benefits costs as % of payroll | $\dfrac{\text{Cost of Benefits}}{\text{Total Payroll}}$ |
|  | Average Total Yrly Compensation/ Exempt Employee | $\dfrac{\text{Total Exempt Compensation}}{\text{Total \# Exempt Employees}}$ |
| Cost of Hire | Hiring Cost/ Exempt Employee | $\dfrac{\text{Total Hiring Cost Exempt EEs}}{\text{\# of Exempt Employees HIred}}$ |

# B. HR METRICS AND DASHBOARDS
## other metrics of various classification:

## Acquisition

- ❏ Cost per hire
- ❏ Time to fill jobs
- ❏ Total Number of New Hires
- ❏ Total number of replacement staff
- ❏ Quality of new hires

## Financial

- ❏ Total labor cost as a percentage of operating expense
- ❏ Average pay per employee
- ❏ Benefits cost as a percent of pay
- ❏ Average performance score as compared to revenue per FTE

## Retention

- ❏ Total separation rate
- ❏ Percentage of voluntary separation to total separations
- ❏ Separations by length of service
- ❏ Percentage of separations among "key" performers
- ❏ Cost of turnover

## Development

- ❏ Training cost as a percentage of payroll
- ❏ Total training hours provided
- ❏ Average number of hours of training per FTE
- ❏ Training hours by functions
- ❏ Training ROI

## Service

- ❏ Employee Satisfaction levels
- ❏ Management Satisfaction levels
- ❏ Percentage of transactions using ESS

## Process/Quality

- ❏ Accuracy in data recording
- ❏ Response time per request

# B. HR METRICS AND DASHBOARDS

**Here are four "rules" of choosing and presenting effective Metrics.**

❑ To have meaning, metrics should have a baseline value and a target value to be compared to.

❑ What gets measured, gets done.

❑ Critical metrics have an owner.

❑ Organizations measure what they treasure.

# C. HR'S INVOLVEMENT IN WORKFORCE CYBER AWARENESS

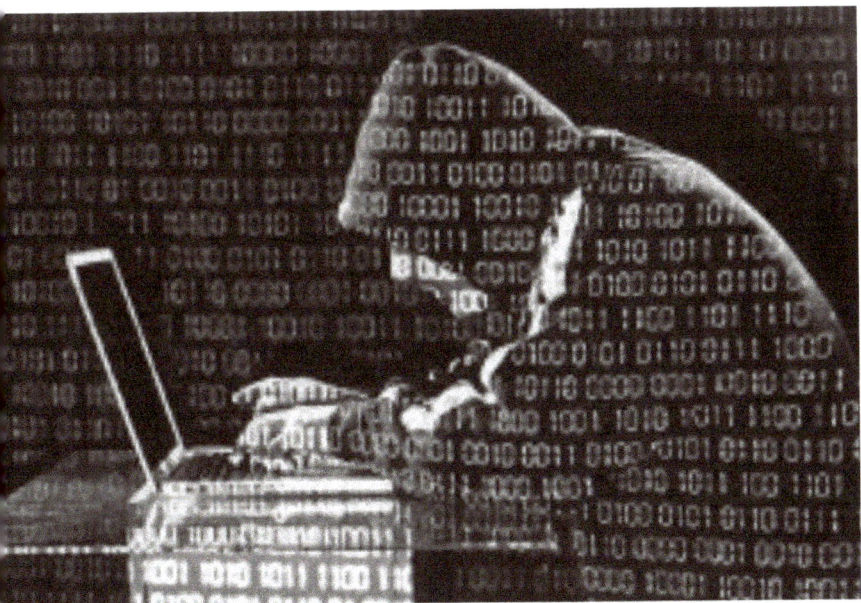

# C. HR'S INVOLVEMENT IN WORK-FORCE CYBER AWARENESS

**The following pages present a recommended initiative that HRJob can co-lead on, with IT and Security and why.**

❑ HR has always had an important role in managing RISKs – from natural disasters to layoff, lawsuits, and workplace violence – and cyber risk is no different – HR has an important role to play.

❑ Cybersecurity is no longer just an Information Technology (IT) issue; it is an enterprise wide issue with implications for everyone.

❑ **"An organization's greatest vulnerability remains it's own workforce"** (Verizon 2015 Data Breach Investigations Report)

# C. HR'S INVOLVEMENT IN WORK-FORCE CYBER AWARENESS

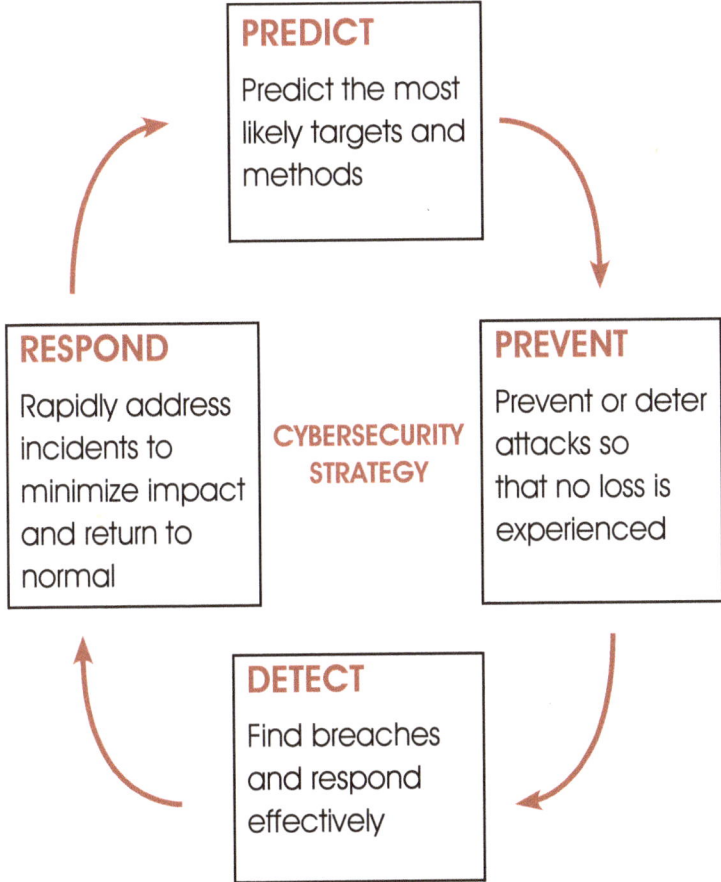

## PREDICT
Predict the most likely targets and methods

## RESPOND
Rapidly address incidents to minimize impact and return to normal

**CYBERSECURITY STRATEGY**

## PREVENT
Prevent or deter attacks so that no loss is experienced

## DETECT
Find breaches and respond effectively

**55% of organizations do not include security awareness in employee performance**

**56% of organizations say that BREACHES are caused by employee carelessness**

# C. HR'S INVOLVEMENT IN WORK-FORCE CYBER AWARENESS

**HR professionals play a critical role: managing aspects of escalation, operational, financial, reputational, and legal risks through effective workforce planning, training and management.**

❑ Security is a continuous cycle in building the TRUST of the workforce.

❑ Technology and Human Behaviors have to be in alignment.

❑ **Workforce Culture** must change.

❑ Obstacles and Opposition need to be recognized and dealt with via a specific **Workforce Awareness Strategic Plan.**

**In all of the above, Human Resources is DIRECTLY INVOLVED.**

# C. HR'S INVOLVEMENT IN WORK-FORCE CYBER AWARENESS

HR must lead, advocate and effectively oversee and communicate the importance of mindfullness of cybersecurity to the entire workforce.

## THE FIVE AREAS OF HR'S INFLUENCE

KNOWLEDGE OF THE WORKFORCE

DELIVERY OF CYBER AWARENESS

SUPPORT IN CYBER SECURITY HIRING

HR'S INVOLVEMENT

UNDERSTANDING AND ADMIN OF WORKFORCE RIGHTS

MANAGEMENT OF HRMS USAGE and PROTECTING HR DATA

# C. HR'S INVOLVEMENT IN WORK-FORCE CYBER AWARENESS

## KNOWLEDGE OF THE WORKFORCE

### HR must:

- ❏ effectively vet new employees.

- ❏ insist on additional scrutiny for all employees in sensitive roles or access to sensitive systems – based on the business "Need to Know."

- ❏ reinforce peer awareness of suspicious behaviors; encourage anonymous and online initiation.

- ❏ carefully configure Cybersecurity work teams.

# C. HR'S INVOLVEMENT IN WORK-FORCE CYBER AWARENESS

## HR must:

- ❑ build specific cybersecurity related job descriptions and then postings.

- ❑ work with IT to select the best candidates; and seek consensus of IT and Cybersecurity managers who have the opening.

- ❑ act aggressively in hiring, as the demand is high and the labor pool is minimal. When possible, utlize executive recruiters and focused recruiters specializing in cyber positions.

- ❑ reach out to the next Generation (Generation Y) who have been trained in high tech campus laboratories.

# C. HR'S INVOLVEMENT IN WORK-FORCE CYBER AWARENESS

**MANAGEMENT OF HRMS USAGE and PROTECTING HR DATA**

## HR must:

- ❑ ensure that the ENTIRE workforce is trained on Cybersecurity procedures: then focus on the use of Employee Self Service and Manager Self Service (ESS/MSS) as provided by the HRMS software provider (or built internally).

- ❑ ensure the rules of access to employee data is based on "need to know."

- ❑ ensure that workflow and report distribution also adheres to the same principle of "need to know" along with security levels and corporate roles.

- ❑ be aware of, and continuously communicate with the primary HRMS software provider about their own back-up and security procedures.

- ❑ do the same with any providers of third party interfaces involved with the HRMS's delivered processes and functionaltiy.

# C. HR'S INVOLVEMENT IN WORK-FORCE CYBER AWARENESS

**MANAGEMENT OF HRMS USAGE and PROTECTING HR DATA**

## HR must:

- ❑ be cautious of SHARING employee data and/or allowing access to your HRMS master file by any THIRD PARTY PROVIDER

- ❑ be aware that you might inherit the security or lack thereof of third party providers.

- ❑ in general, apply enhanced enterprise wide security standards: frequent password change requirements, along with password strength rules, data classification levels, encryption, backups and access controls.

- ❑ consider implementing MULTI-FACTOR authentication and move towards biometrics, at a minimum – fingerprint scanning.

# C. HR'S INVOLVEMENT IN WORK-FORCE CYBER AWARENESS

## UNDERSTANDING AND ADMIN OF WORKFORCE RIGHTS

### HR must:

❑ involve Legal to review gathering and storage practices for hiring data.

❑ be aware of geographic regulations that differ for employee data security and any cross-border data transfer issues.

❑ ensure that Privacy controls extend to employees, vendors, customers, contract consultants and other business partners.

❑ be prepared for electronic discovery requests from government agencies and have communications and chain of command procedures in place.

❑ understand when data breach notices are required and work with Legal and Public Relations when issuing them.

❑ be aware of US (and other countries) laws concerning hiring interviews (discrimination) and background checks (legality and notice).

# C. HR'S INVOLVEMENT IN WORK-FORCE CYBER AWARENESS

## DELIVERY OF CYBER AWARENESS

**HR's workforce management strategy and it's Cybersecurity initiatives must be aligned to deliver cyber awareness by:**

- ❑ defining and documenting policies that explain the enterprise-wide accepted level of risk and regulatory compliance.

- ❑ requiring regular and documented attendance/completion of delivered Cybersecurity awareness training.

- ❑ providing continuous ad-hoc updates as needed.

- ❑ communicating the seriousness of all aspects of being aware of Cybersecurity.

- ❑ reinforcing a culture of mindfulness and awareness and the need to report suspicious behaviors.

# C. HR'S INVOLVEMENT IN WORK-FORCE CYBER AWARENESS

## A workforce optimized for cyber security is described as this:

- ❑ The people responsible for tools and technology are given proper (but limited) authorities to access and protect data and systems.

- ❑ The organization has the right governance structure to balance its business objectives with security needs as part of overall enterprise risk management.

- ❑ The organization has clear and broad consensus on the cyber security risks that are most important to the business and industry in which it operates.

- ❑ Security is a broadly understood priority, with leaders building a cyber security culture where the right behaviors are actually encouraged.

- ❑ The right people—with the right competencies and capabilities—are available to support the enterprise. They are deployed to the right places within the organizational structure.

- ❑ The entire workforce is doing the right things to be resistant to exploitation of human vulnerabilities, which typically represent the biggest risk to any organization.

# C. HR'S INVOLVEMENT IN WORK-FORCE CYBER AWARENESS

## Recommendations for HR to ensure a cyber aware workforce:

☐ Actively participate in the Cybersecurity planning process.

☐ Ensure appropriate leaders from IT, Operations, Legal and Finance are involved.

☐ Seek the support of senior leadership.

☐ Establish a cross functional committee to build policies.

☐ Ensure workforce planning considers all roles in the organization:

♦ Technical, non-technical, management, third party vendors.

☐ Issue new stringent PASSWORD CHANGE requirements – INCLUDING PENALTIES AND TRACKING INDIVIDUAL COMPLIANCE AT EVERY LEVEL.

☐ Instill a culture of peer to peer vigilance, communicate that it is ok to be watchful of colleague behaviors.

# D.

**VENDORS WHO SUPPORT BUILDING CLOUT via "CAREER MANAGEMENT" FUNCTIONALITY**

# D. VENDORS WHO SUPPORT BUILDING **CLOUT** via "CAREER MANAGEMENT" FUNCTIONALITY

❑ When **"Talent Management Software"** is Googled, various industry analyst reports and buyers guides list nearly 200 software providers within this broad category. Many are familiar as top tier full functioned HRMS, such as Workday, SAP/SuccessFactors and Oracle HCM Cloud. These providers of HR technology deliver distinct modules – well integrated with their applicant tracking and recruiting functionality within the overall HRMS database structure.

❑ Additionally, among the nearly 200, are vendors whose sole focus is on Talent Management or Career Management in support of goals and objectives of individual employees. Among those known by me and seemingly well respected are:

> Cornerstone OnDemand (PiiQ), Halogen Talent Space, PeopleFluent, Saba Software, Insala, TalentGuard

❑ See for yourself: these are good listings of "Talent Management" or Career Management" software providers:

- ♦ Captera.com
- ♦ SoftwareAdvice.com

# D. VENDORS WHO SUPPORT BUILDING **CLOUT** via "CAREER MANAGEMENT" FUNCTIONALITY

**However, and Importantly, more recently a few newer software providers whose focus is more on the career path/ladder progression for each employee and who incorporate Organizational Behavior and Industrial Psychology concepts have entered the marketplace.** They deliver interactive content – some using "gamification" techniques, over attractively delivered apps for smartphones and tablets. They place the overall employee experience, engagment and career progression directly into the hands of the employee first, and the manager second. As of now, these are stand alone applications but many have already integrated their capabilities within underlying HRMS systems of record. The vendors who are leading the movement are:

- ❑ **CULTURE AMP**
- ❑ **FUEL50**
- ❑ **QUANTUM WORKPLACE**

*From each of their websites: here are a few statements about their functionality and approaches...*

# D. VENDORS WHO SUPPORT BUILDING **CLOUT** via "CAREER MANAGEMENT" FUNCTIONALITY

## C Culture Amp

## Culture Amp – www.cultureamp.com

### Approach:

### Modern psychology
Our team of organizational psychologists use our own and other current research to reimagine survey strategy and shape new products.

### Sophisticated analytics
Our data scientists are constantly evolving and adding tools to Culture Amp. The platform automatically surfaces key drivers, and provides text analysis and heat maps.

### Leading technology
We've built an in-house team of the world's leading engineers, product designers and UX specialists to ensure Culture Amp's powerful capability is accessible to everyone.

### "People Geek" community
Our global community explores how data can drive a better world to work in.

# D. VENDORS WHO SUPPORT BUILDING **CLOUT** via "CAREER MANAGEMENT" FUNCTIONALITY

## ◯ Culture Amp

## Culture Amp – www.cultureamp.com

### Products:

**Employee Engagement**
Diagnostic, deep dive and pulse surveys with powerful analytics and action planning.

**Employee Experience**
Create remarkable experiences from interview to exit and beyond. Automated employee surveys for each lifecycle milestone: onboarding, exit and more.

**Employee Effectiveness**
Empower people to drive their own development.

Action-oriented 180° and 360° feedback for managers, individuals and teams.

# D. VENDORS WHO SUPPORT BUILDING **CLOUT** via "CAREER MANAGEMENT" FUNCTIONALITY

## Fuel50 – www.fuel50.com

### Approach:

Fuel50 is award-winning career path software that enables leaders to engage and motivate their teams, and empowers employees to have a visible career pathway within their organization.

**GIVE YOUR PEOPLE THE KEY TO THEIR CAREERS**
Fuel50's career path software empowers employees. Through a range of gamified tools, employees are prompted to think differently and take charge of their careers. Upon completing these exercises, Fuel50 analyses the aspirations, talents, values, skills, and interests of your employees and matches them with career path opportunities within the business. Fuel50 matches employees with internal opportunities while also showing them insightful gap analysis — what they're good at, and what they need to work on.

# D. VENDORS WHO SUPPORT BUILDING **CLOUT** via "CAREER MANAGEMENT" FUNCTIONALITY

## Fuel50 – www.fuel50.com

### Products:

**FOR EMPLOYEES**

Empower your employees to understand their career drivers, create engaging career pathways linked to their roles, and provide goals that are business-aligned to their values and aspirations.

**FOR LEADERS**

Enable your leaders to have simple but powerful career conversations with their people through powerful insights and resources that are delivered across three levels of career engagement coaching.

**FOR ORGANIZATIONS**

Give your HR, OD and leaders clear visibility to employee career drivers, succession risk areas, and engagement levers to support strategic people initiatives and business success.

# D. VENDORS WHO SUPPORT BUILDING **CLOUT** via "CAREER MANAGEMENT" FUNCTIONALITY

QUANTUM WORKPLACE

## Quantum Workplace – www.quantumworkplace.com

### Approach:

An All-in-One Employee Engagement Platform

Quantum Workplace has all the tools you need to turn employee feedback into impact throughout the entire employee experience, plus the services and support to help companies master employee engagement.

# D. VENDORS WHO SUPPORT BUILDING **CLOUT** via "CAREER MANAGEMENT" FUNCTIONALITY

**QUANTUM** WORKPLACE

## Quantum Workplace – www.quantumworkplace.com

### Products:

**EMPLOYEE ENGAGEMENT**

Surveys and Pulses

Analytics

Commitments

**EMPLOYEE PERFORMANCE**

Recognition

Goals

Feedback

One on One conversations

**EMPLOYEE EXITS**

Surveys

Analytics

# TO MY READERS:

**Thank you for your time (and for your purchase!)**

I hope you enjoyed the read and that you feel that you have benefited both personally and professionally from the journey – progressing from the lows of lying on the ground as a victim **(Ms. Harriet Rose Job)**, to the heights of learnings from both Aliens from Outer Space visiting the Earth, and from me - with messages of collaboration and strategic positioning to help you build your own influence and **CLOUT**.

**You are a member of a worldwide group of professionals within the critically important role of Human Resource management,** and should never feel targeted!

**Your feedback is welcome.**

**www.marcsmillerassociates.com**
**Email: marc@marcsmillerassociates.com**

New Yorker, **MARC S. MILLER** is a nationally known thought leader, consultant, speaker and author on many aspects of technology solutions for Human Resources. His consulting firm, Marc S Miller Associates and his industry visibility has made Marc one of the HR Technology industry's most recognized voices.

His creativity and fun attitude has been evidenced at numerous HR and HCM technology meetings both industry focused and at many HRMS providers User Conferences. He is always reachable at marc@marcsmillerassociates.com.